# The Prefabricated Home

# The Prefabricated Home

Colin Davies

REAKTION BOOKS

Published by Reaktion Books Ltd
79 Farringdon Road
London EC1M 3JU, UK

www.reaktionbooks.co.uk

First published 2005, reprinted 2005

Printed and bound in Great Britain
by Cromwell Press, Trowbridge, Wiltshire

British Library Cataloguing in Publication Data

Davies, Colin
    The prefabricated home
    1. Prefabricated houses  2. Architecture, Domestic – 20th century
    3. Buildings, Prefabricated  4. Architecture, Modern – 20th century
    I. Title
    728.3'7'09045

    ISBN 1 86189 243 8

# Contents

When I was younger
It was plain to me
I must make something of myself.
Older now
I walk back streets
Admiring the houses
Of the very poor . . .

from *Pastoral* by William Carlos Williams

# Introduction

This is a book about the prefabricated house, but more importantly it is a book about modern architecture. The idea is that a study of the prefabricated house might shed light on the true nature of modern architecture and show the way forward to its much-needed reform.

'Architecture' in this book doesn't just mean the design of buildings. It refers to something broader and vaguer: a 'field' in which people compete for cultural and social capital. The architecture field includes everything to do with architecture: values, ideologies, specialized skills, jargon, codes of conduct, professional institutions, education, history, books, exhibitions, networks of patronage, prominent personalities, mythical heroes and canonical buildings. The idea of architecture as a field, rather than a profession or a discipline, comes from a book called *The Favored Circle* by Garry Stevens, who borrowed the general concept of the field from the French sociologist Pierre Bourdieu.[1]

Anyone familiar with the architecture field can say with some certainty what is included and what is not. For example, a semi-detached suburban London house built in the 1930s probably doesn't count as architecture, but the back extension to the house, designed by a newly qualified architect with the passion that only a first commission can arouse, probably does. On the other hand people who are called architects might sometimes find themselves excluded from the architecture field. The design of the British Iron and Steel Federation house of the late 1940s, for example, has been attributed to Frederick Gibberd, a famous architect, but this does not disqualify it from inclusion in the *non-architectural* history of the prefabricated house. One of the advantages of the concept of the field is that it gives critics and historians room to manoeuvre. The boundary between the architectural and the non-architectural can be gerrymandered to suit the argument. Nevertheless most people will allow that what is untrue in a narrow professional sense can be true in a broader cultural sense.

Why should the prefabricated house be the key to the reform of modern architecture? Because, although we think of architecture as being in some sense in charge of the activity of building, for 150 years or more the prefabricated house has managed perfectly well without architecture's guidance. Situated outside the architecture field, it has cheerfully ignored architectural law. The strength of the prefabricated house lies in its popularity, its cheapness and the industrial base from which it operates. These are precisely the areas in which modern architecture is weakest. Modern architecture is unpopular, expensive and divorced from industrial production. This is why whenever it has tried to extend its field to include the territory of the prefabricated house it has failed and been forced to retreat.

Art and construction are also fields. One of the curious characteristics of the architecture field is that it is more closely allied with art than with construction. In the introduction to his *Outline of European Architecture*, first published in 1942, the great Modernist architectural historian Nikolaus Pevsner defines architecture in purely artistic terms. Painters, he says, deal with line and colour, sculptors deal with form, and architects deal with space. There are some obvious objections to this idea that the architect is an artist not too different from a painter or sculptor, such as the fact that buildings are useful objects, more like bridges or boats than paintings or statues. Architecture and construction, which one might assume to be very close, actually have very little in common. Architects and builders may be able to rub along together on a professional level but culturally they are worlds apart. They speak different languages, they have different aims and different tastes, they are educated differently and they have different histories.

In the developed world the great majority of buildings, perhaps 80 per cent by value, are not designed by architects and fall outside the architecture field. Yet inside the architecture field, in schools of architecture for example, it is normal to speak and act as if all buildings were designed by architects. It is a fiction tacitly maintained to preserve the illusion that architecture is a real force for change in the world. Ironically, this self-delusion is one of the reasons why architecture is at present *not* a real force for change in the world. Most of the non-architectural 80 per cent of buildings are houses. Very few ordinary houses count as architecture. This is another of architecture's guilty secrets: that it fails to have any effect on most people's most intimate experience of buildings. Combine this with the widening gulf between architecture and construction and you can begin to see why the prefabricated house is architecture's biggest challenge.

Prefabrication is nothing new. Parts of buildings have been made in factories for at least 200 years. Machine-made bricks, ceramic tiles, sawn timber, sheet glass, sash windows, cast-iron columns and beams – all were familiar factory-made products in nineteenth-century Europe and America. Whole buildings – houses, hospitals, churches, factories, barracks – were made in kit form and shipped to colonies and war zones all over the world. Twentieth-century examples include the mobile home, the post-war British 'prefab' and container cabins for offshore oil workers.

But the relationship between architecture and prefabrication has always been problematic. Architects have found it hard to come to terms with the idea that the products of their art might be made in a factory. This is not surprising, perhaps. When the industrial revolution first stirred, architecture was already an ancient craft. Some have seen architecture as a bulwark of resistance against industrial culture, maintaining eternal values in a world driven mad by what money can buy. 'When we build,' said John Ruskin, 'let us think that we build for ever.' In the nineteenth century architecture remained aloof from industry, concerning itself with churches, art galleries and town halls while ignoring factories, railway sheds and urban housing for the poor. But then in the early years of the twentieth century it seemed that architecture and industry might be reconciled. Progressive architects in France and Germany tried to create a new architecture that would use the products of industry while teaching industry about art. Stripped of all traditional ornament, the new Modernist architecture would be the very embodiment of a reformed industrial world.

The early Modernists put the prefabricated house at the centre of their programme of reform. Architectural history may pretend otherwise, but the fact is that their prefabricated house projects all failed. Some architects interpret this as a failure of the prefabricated house *per se*, a proof that buildings do not lend themselves to factory production. But this is not true. Millions of successful prefabricated houses have been built all over the world, but architectural history ignores them because they are beyond the pale of the architecture field. While architecture has been struggling to find the true artistic expression of industrial production, construction has been quietly industrializing itself behind architecture's back.

Why should this matter? Architecture failed to change the world, but so what? No one seems to mind very much. Why not just accept that society expects some buildings, like art galleries and skyscrapers, to be architecture, but is content for other buildings, like ordinary houses, to be non-architecture? The usual answer, spoken from inside the architecture field, is that the quality of the built environment would be so much higher if architects were allowed to design more of it. But it is common knowledge that architects' architecture is often disliked by non-architects. So the argument quickly shifts its ground: in that case the general public should learn to appreciate good architecture. It is all a question of education. We need visual awareness classes in primary schools and preliminary architecture courses in secondary schools. In other words, the world will have to change to suit architecture, not vice versa. But architecture has already tried and failed to reshape the world in its own image. Its chances of succeeding now are virtually nil.

So why should anybody care about the relationship between architecture and the prefabricated house? One reason is that the presence of an exclusive architecture field creams off design talent from the rest of building. Intelligent school-leavers with an interest in building go to college to study architecture. It is a popular course. Few people want to be project managers or surveyors or structural engineers, but lots of people want to be architects. And when those intelligent school-leavers begin their architecture courses they are immediately immersed in the values of the architecture field. They learn that to compete successfully for cultural and social capital they must identify themselves exclusively with the architecture field and not be tempted to stray into the neighbouring construction field. The result is that 80 per cent of building is starved of design talent.

It is likely, in view of the above remarks, that this book will be interpreted as an attack on the architectural profession. But this is not the intention. The architecture field feeds many foolish vanities but at its heart lies a genuine love of building. Architecture is about more than just the development of products for a market. It is about space and place, home and community, body and memory, earth and sky. It is for people, for their whole lives, not just their lives as consumers. The architecture field should grow, not shrink. But first it must reform itself. The intention of this book is to suggest some of the ways in which architecture might re-engage with its hinterland, with its customers, with its colleagues in the construction industry and with the general public. The prefabricated house has been chosen as a vehicle for this discussion partly because it is a subject of wide current interest but mainly because it challenges architecture's most deep-seated prejudices. It calls into question the concept of authorship, which is central to architecture's view of itself as an art form; it insists on a knowledge of production methods, marketing and distribution as well as construction; it disallows architecture's normal obsession with the needs of individual clients and the specific qualities of particular places; and its lightweight, portable technologies mock architecture's monumental pretensions. But if architecture could adapt itself to these conditions and succeed in the prefabricated house business, then it might recover some of the influence it has lost in the last 30 years and begin to make a real difference to the quality of the built environment. That is the point that this book is trying to make.

# 1. An architectural history

The prefabricated house is an important theme, perhaps the most important, in the conventional, canonical history of twentieth-century architecture. Architectural history favours the movement known as Modernism, which had its origins before the First World War and is honoured still, though sometimes indirectly, in our post-modernist world. Modernists rejected the élitism, historicism and anti-industrialism that had characterized their profession in the nineteenth century. They wanted to bring architecture to the masses and to face up to the realities of an industrial society. What better way to achieve this goal than to design houses that would be mass-produced in factories, just like Model T Fords?

The most important figure in the early history of the architect-designed, prefabricated house is undoubtedly Charles-Edouard Jeanneret-Gris, better known as Le Corbusier. He is important both as a brilliantly inventive designer and as a gifted propagandist in the Modernist cause. His book *Vers une architecture*, mainly a collection of articles from the magazine *L'Esprit nouveau*, which he edited with the painter Amédée Ozenfant, was and is a publishing phenomenon. It has run into countless editions and reprints and has been an inspiration to architects ever since it was first published in 1923. The first English translation, under the title *Towards a New Architecture*, appeared in 1927 and is still in print.[1] The last but one chapter of the book is entitled 'Mass Production Houses'. It is very short, less than 2,000 words, but padded out with drawings and extended captions describing an impressive array of Le Corbusier's own designs for mass production houses.

First comes the famous Dom-Ino house of 1914, illustrated by a little perspective drawing of three flat floor slabs supported by six columns and linked by a cantilevered concrete stair. The idea was that these units would be mass-produced, lined up on the site like dominoes on a table and infilled with blockwork walls and standard doors and windows to make cheap, flexible dwellings. The resulting linear blocks, illustrated in perspective sketches,

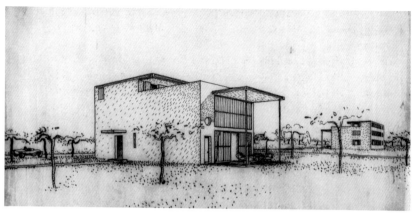

Le Corbusier, perspective drawing of Maison Citrohan, 1920.

look advanced for their time, with big, factory-style windows, sometimes turning the corner of a block where in traditional load-bearing wall construction you would expect to find a solid pier, but they do not look mass-produced. There is no sense of the house as a complete, factory-made unit, like a car. Similarly, the 'Monol' house system of 1919, with its asbestos-cased rubble walls and curved concrete roof, is more an ingenious way to eliminate the cost and inconvenience of transporting heavy building materials than a true mass-produced house.

When we come to the Maison Citrohan of 1920, however, the image of the mass-produced house suddenly comes into focus. Without knowing anything about the construction of this house we can see immediately that it is meant to be a standardized product. The perspective view shows two identical detached houses, differently orientated so as to show us all four elevations, in a spacious suburban setting. And the name Citrohan, a slightly obscure pun on Citroën, the car-maker, seems to indicate that the house is not just standardized but also mass-produced in a factory. Le Corbusier designed several versions of the Maison Citrohan, but all of them have a double-height living-room lit by a big window almost filling one wall. One possible prototype for this room is the traditional Parisian artist's studio, though the direct inspiration seems to have been a bistro that Le Corbusier and Ozenfant used to frequent in the rue Godot-de-Mauroy.[2] In the earliest version the kitchen is on the ground floor at the back, the master bedroom is on the first floor with a balcony overlooking the living-room, and the children's or guests' bedrooms are on the top floor, where there is also a large roof terrace. All this is contained in the simplest possible envelope – basically a box, with no concessions to traditional domestic forms: no gables or bay windows or rustic porches, certainly no ornament. Form and plan are meant to suggest both a new way of life and a new method of house production.

The comparison between the Maison Citrohan and an automobile is, however, rather misleading. Le Corbusier may have intended these houses to be 'mass produced', but it is doubtful if he ever envisaged them being made in a factory. In the early versions the basic structure is of load-bearing 'cross walls', built on site in materials to suit the region, with concrete floors spanning between. In later versions the whole house is lifted off the ground on concrete columns or 'pilotis', which implies a reinforced concrete frame. A caption describes it as: 'Framework of concrete, girders made on the site and raised by a hand winch'. The phrase 'mass-produced' in English implies factory production, but the title of the chapter in French is 'Maisons en séries', which carries no such overtone. Whenever he talked about industrializing the building process, Le Corbusier seemed to envisage a rationalization of the building site rather than a shift of operations into the factory, at least as far as the basic structure of the building was concerned.

One aspect of this rationalization was the standardization of components. Standardization, for Le Corbusier, was a philosophical and artistic as much as a practical concept. He was a painter as well as an architect, and the co-founder with Ozenfant of a movement (or would-be movement) known as Purism. In the typical Purist painting, for example Le Corbusier's *Still-life with a Pile of Plates* (1920), everyday objects – plates, bottles, clay pipes, a book, a guitar – are depicted so as to emphasize their generic rather than their specific qualities. The plates are circular and shown as if in plan, the book is solidified as if it were carved from stone, and the pipes are combinations of perfect cylinders. What the Purists liked about these objects was that they seemed to have developed over a very long period, finally arriving at a perfect, or pure, or typical form. They were, in the Purist jargon, *objets-types* and as such they were considered to have a natural beauty. On the face of it this idea has nothing to do with industrial production. None of the objects is a new invention. On the contrary, they all seem to be profoundly traditional. Invented objects or machines such as typewriters or phonographs seem to have been deliberately excluded. But in Le Corbusier's thinking the *objet-type* became confused with the idea of industrial production. The new industrial age would, he hoped, also produce objects of natural beauty, refined and perfected not by centuries of craft and human use, but by market competition:

All motor cars have the same essential arrangements. But, by reason of the unceasing competition between the innumerable firms who make them,

Le Corbusier, *Still-life with a Pile of Plates*, 1920, oil on canvas.

every maker has found himself obliged to get to the top of this competition and, over and above the standard of practical realisation, to prosecute the search for a perfection and a harmony beyond the mere practical side, a manifestation not only of perfection and harmony but of beauty.[3]

If only buildings, and especially houses, could be subjected to the same astringent influences, then they too would become naturally beautiful, like motor cars, and like the *objets-types* in the paintings. But there is a double misunderstanding here. First, the forms of invented industrial products like automobiles are arrived at by a process radically different from that which produced the *objets-types*. It might be possible to argue that plates and bottles are mass-produced and that this must influence their form, but what about the book and the guitar? These are pre-industrial forms, 'given' rather than invented. Second, why should it be assumed that industrial production tends to produce beautiful objects (in Le Corbusier's terms) when it was already perfectly obvious by 1923, indeed had been perfectly obvious since 1851, when the Crystal Palace had been filled with the gaudy fruits of the first phase of the industrial revolution, that if anything the opposite was true: industrial production tended to produce tasteless tat. Furthermore, industrial production and the market

Le Corbusier, Immeubles-Villas project, 1922.

tend to value novelty of form more than perfection of form. The process of invention does not stop when the typical form is reached. If it did the market would stagnate.

Le Corbusier's thinking about the relationship between design and industrial production was, then, rather muddled. Looking again at the form of the Maison Citrohan in the light of Purist theory, it seems to have more to do with vernacular architecture than with design for industrial production. Many historians have remarked on its resemblance to traditional Mediterranean houses – the plain white walls, the flat roof and (in some versions) the external staircase. If it were not called the Maison Citrohan, if it were not an illustration in a chapter entitled 'Mass Production Houses', we might almost interpret it as a nostalgic attempt to recover the simplicity and purity of a pre-industrial age.

Le Corbusier was in fact profoundly influenced by certain traditional building types, in particular the monastery, and specifically the Carthusian monastery at Galluzzo, near Florence, which he visited in 1907. The monks were each provided with an individual cell and a little walled garden, but the cells and gardens were arranged around the perimeter of a communal cloister. This perfect balance between community and privacy deeply impressed Le Corbusier and remained with him as a design principle for the rest of his life. His first clear application of this principle was in a project he called 'Immeubles-Villas', fully illustrated in *Towards a New Architecture*, where the name is translated as 'Freehold Maisonettes'. It is basically an eight-storey block of flats, with communal sports and entertainment facilities on the roof and a great covered court 'for tennis'. But what is truly original about it is that the flats have two storeys, with double-height living-rooms like the Maison Citrohan,

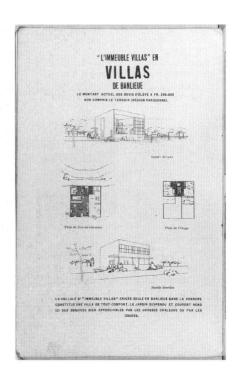

The Pavillon de l'Esprit Nouveau marketed as a suburban house, from the *Almanach d'architecture moderne*, 1923.

and have not just a balcony, but a sizeable garden to one side. They are conceived as individual houses with gardens, piled up to form a multi-storey block. Le Corbusier actually built a single Immeuble-Villa at the Paris Exposition Internationale des Arts Décoratifs et Industriels Modernes of 1925. Called the Pavillon de l'Esprit Nouveau, after the magazine, it was sponsored by the Voisin car and aeroplane company. In the exhibition literature there was an attempt to market the villa as an individual suburban house. Meanwhile, in an adjacent structure Le Corbusier's visionary urban projects, the Ville Contemporaine and the Plan Voisin, were exhibited, showing versions of the villa in its mass housing form. Here then, neatly encapsulated, was a theoretical solution to the whole dilemma of individual houses versus mass housing with which politicians, designers and builders have struggled ever since.

The Maison Citrohan and its derivatives were realized in various forms over the next 30 years. In 1927 a version was constructed at the Weissenhofsiedlung in Stuttgart, a permanent exhibition organized by the Deutscher Werkbund for which almost every prominent Modernist architect built a house. Far from being a cheap, mass-produced object, the Weissenhof Citrohan was hand crafted and far more expensive than any other house in the exhibition. In 1929 a development

The Weissenhof version of the Maison Citrohan.

of 51 workers' houses was completed at Pessac for the eccentric industrialist Henri Frugès. The basic Citrohan elements were standardized and assembled in different combinations to form two- and three-storey semi-detached and terraced houses. Construction was rationalized, using a 5 by 2.5-metre planning grid, but not in any real sense factory produced, and there were considerable problems with the innovative sprayed concrete technology. The stark appearance of the houses caused outrage. Frugès himself cheerfully reported that most of the people attending the opening ceremony thought he had gone mad. No one wanted to live in the houses and they were eventually let to very poor tenants who set about adapting them in a most creative way, making them more like conventional houses by moving partitions, filling in the pilotis, adding pitched roofs and shortening the ribbon windows. The estate was restored and gentrified in the 1980s.

The Citrohan aesthetic recruited its admirers from the intellectual bourgeoisie rather than the working class. In 1926 Gabrielle de Monzie, the estranged wife of the politician Anatole de Monzie, and her millionaire friends Michael and Sarah Stein (relations of Gertrude Stein) commissioned Le Corbusier to design a villa in the Paris suburb of Vaucresson. The Villa Stein-de Monzie is

Housing at Pessac by Le Corbusier, photographed in 1971.

four storeys high with a complicated arrangement of spaces, interpenetrating horizontally and vertically but all contained in a rectangular frame, like a Purist painting. But with its plain white walls, its ribbon windows, roof garden and Immeuble-Villa-like, two-storey covered terrace, it is still recognizably of the Citrohan family. We can see features of the Maison Citrohan in all of Le Corbusier's 1920s villas: the Villa La Roche, the Villa Cook and even, though less obviously, in the Villa Savoye of 1930.

Twenty years later the Citrohan prototype reappears in the famous Unité d'Habitation in Marseilles, the massive housing block that was the inspiration for so many high-rise estates of the 1960s and '70s. The Unité apartments are very narrow and extend right across the building so that they face two ways. On one side only they are two storeys high, so as to accommodate the familiar Citrohan device of the double-height living space. For a time during the development of the design it was envisaged that the flats would be mass-produced in a factory and slotted into the structural frame like bottles in a wine rack. Jean Prouvé, architect, inventor and designer of prefabricated houses, prepared outline proposals for a version in steel, but it came to nothing and the block was eventually constructed conventionally from *in situ* reinforced concrete.

Le Corbusier was the most important European architect of the twentieth century. In the years after the Second World War the architecture that grew from those early projects for mass-produced houses became a new orthodoxy that transformed the cities of the developed world. And yet in its original aim – the production of cheap, individual houses for working people – it was a complete failure. Le Corbusier's influence on publicly funded mass housing was enormous, but his influence on the individual house for sale on the open market was virtually nil. Whenever people had a choice, they rejected the Modernist aesthetic, always preferring a traditional image. Le Corbusier never did realize his dream of the factory-made house.

*The Dream of the Factory-made House* is the title of a book by Gilbert Herbert, published in 1984.[4] It mainly tells the story of a collaboration in the 1940s between two emigré German architects on a project to design and manufacture a mass-produced 'Packaged House' for the American market. You can tell from the title that the story does not have a happy ending. The dream did not come true. A factory was set up designed for a minimum output of 10,000 houses a year. In the event, fewer than 200 were produced and only a handful were actually sold. The project was a disastrous failure. The curious thing about Herbert's book is that, although a work of exemplary scholarship, it never really explains why the project failed. It is as if Herbert cannot quite believe that it did. He wants it to succeed and he gives it a tremendous build up over nine chapters, tracing the careers of his two protagonists right back over 30 years or more. Then, in chapter ten, he is finally forced to submit to historical fact and deliver his tragic ending.

And you can understand his frustration. The two architects were Konrad Wachsmann, who was to go on to claim a place in architectural history as a pioneer of space-frame structures, and Walter Gropius, the founder of the famous Bauhaus school and a giant figure in the history of Modernism. It is hard to think of any two architects active in the US in 1942 who were better equipped to make a success of such a project. Wachsmann was originally trained as a craftsman, a cabinetmaker, before attending art schools in Berlin and Dresden to study under famous teachers like Heinrich Tessenow and Hans Poelzig. It was Poelzig who, in 1926, got Wachsmann a job in the design office of Europe's biggest timber building manufacturer, Christoph and Unmack. Within a few months Wachsmann had been made chief designer and had set about rationalizing the company's design and marketing operations. When, in 1929, he read that Albert Einstein was to be offered a country home by the city of Berlin, he managed to persuade Einstein and his wife to choose a Christoph and Unmack house. Having pulled off this spectacular public relations coup and successfully completed the house to the Einsteins' satisfaction, he left the company to set up his own architectural practice. Unusually for an architect, therefore, Wachsmann had direct experience both of making things with his own hands and of the factory production of buildings. It was an experience that was to colour his architectural outlook for the rest of his life. In 1930 he wrote a book called *Holzhausbau* (quite recently translated into English under the title *Building the Wooden House*)[5] in which he summarized what he had learnt under three headings: 'The On Site Wood Frame Method', 'The Panel Method' and 'The Log House Method'. A large part of the book is devoted to beautiful black-and-white photographs of simple, practical buildings – houses, schools, children's homes, hotels – which still, perhaps now more than ever, have the power to inspire architects of the more modest and sensitive kind.

Walter Gropius was even better equipped than Wachsmann to make a success of the Packaged House project. He was one of the 'form givers' of European Modernist architecture. He founded the Bauhaus, the most influential art school of the twentieth century, and ran it successfully for nine years. When the Bauhaus moved from Weimar to Dessau in 1927, Gropius designed a building to house it that has been recognized ever since as the first masterpiece of the new style. Where Wachsmann was volatile and rebellious, Gropius was correct and reliable in all his dealings and had a calm, aristocratic bearing. The painter Paul Klee called him 'the Silver Prince', an appellation that was to be repeated with a sneer by Tom Wolfe in his 1981 anti-modernist tract *From Bauhaus to our House*.[6] Gropius had been interested in the idea of mass-produced houses since 1910, when he had presented a detailed proposal for the setting up of a housing production company to the president of the German industrial giant, AEG (see Chapter 6). In 1927 he had built a demonstration prefabricated house – a stark, steel-framed box – at the Weissenhofsiedlung housing exhibition in Stuttgart. And in 1931/2 he had worked with the Hirsch Copper and Brass company, helping to develop a copper-clad panel housing system and lending it architectural respectability before the project was overtaken by economic and political events in Germany.

Gropius left Germany in 1934. After a brief stay in England, where he collaborated with the architect Maxwell Fry on several projects, he arrived in America in 1937 and walked straight into a job as the head of the school of architecture at Harvard University. Wachsmann's arrival in America in 1941 was very different. Penniless and destitute, he found refuge with Gropius and his wife in their house in Lincoln, Massachusetts. It was there that the packaged house idea was born. With no job and nothing to do, Wachsmann set about developing his idea for an industrialized panel-based building system that would make the products of Cristoph and Unmack look primitive. He concentrated most of his effort on the development of a jointing system that would allow two-, three- and four-way connections between panels. All the main elements of the building – external walls, partitions, floors, ceilings and roofs – would be assembled from versions of the same basic wooden panel. Meanwhile Gropius, the 'godfather' of the enterprise, set about applying for

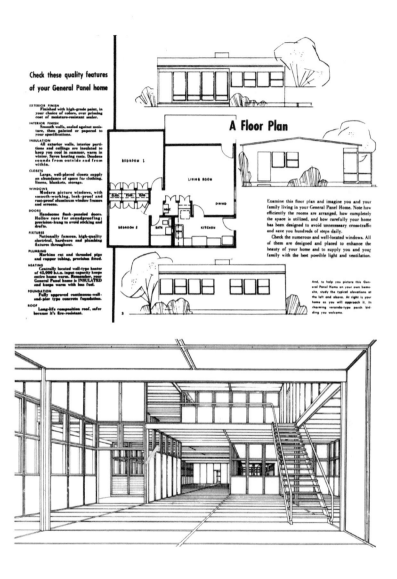

Marketing brochure for the Packaged House by Gropius and Wachsmann.
Perspective drawing of the Packaged House system.

patents, cultivating his contacts and arranging finance. In February 1942 the National Housing Agency allocated $153 million for the housing of displaced defence workers with a production target of 42,000 houses. Gropius himself might have had some influence on this policy, having presented a paper on the subject to the House Select Committee investigating National Migration in 1941. Conditions could hardly have been more favourable for the development of a prefabricated housing system. In September 1942 the General Panel Corporation was set up to make the Packaged House and a few months later a demonstration house was built, which Gropius proudly showed to groups of important government officials. The house was architecturally modest, not to say dull: single-storey, with a straightforward rectangular plan, a shallow pitched roof and an inset porch. But it was the abstract qualities of the house that were impressive, its uniformity and precision. The important officials were duly impressed, a marketing campaign was launched with articles in the professional and lay press, and the future of the project seemed assured. But two years later, in May 1945, the war was over and still the company had not produced any houses. Relating this fact, Gilbert Herbert seems beside himself with frustration:

Amazingly, despite the enthusiasm with which it was initiated and pursued, despite the ingenuity of its design, despite the energy of Wachsmann and the reputation of Gropius, despite professional acclaim and government approval, despite its initial Wall Street backing, despite its subsequent linkage with experienced industrial management, despite all this it had missed the entire phase of wartime demand.[7]

There was, however, a second chance. Millions of houses were still needed, not for defence workers this time, but for GIs returning from the war. In February 1946 a Veterans Emergency Housing programme was set up. Factories that had made armaments for war would now make houses and government grants were available. There was a shake-up in the management structure of the General Panel Corporation, more capital was raised and the former Lockheed Factory in Burbank, California, was acquired. By this time Gropius had taken a back seat, but Wachsmann set about the design of the factory production line with all the energy and enthusiasm that he had brought to the design of the product itself. A lot of sophisticated and expensive machinery was installed including 'high frequency presses', which could cure glued joints in seconds. By the middle of 1947 everything was ready. But it was too late. The Veterans Emergency Housing programme had been cancelled and the government had withdrawn its support. The factory was reduced to making doors and scenery flats for Hollywood movies. The Packaged House had missed the boat. Again.

But why? The enterprise was probably under-financed, the management structure of the company was divided between New York and California, leading to duplications and misunderstandings, the houses were too expensive, the terms of government loans were unreasonable – there were, of course, lots of reasons. Perhaps the dream of the factory-made house was destined never to come true. Perhaps the whole idea of mass production is fundamentally alien to the concept 'house', with all its sentimental associations, all its historical and cultural depth. But no. This won't do. The General Panel Corporation was very far from being the only mass-produced house manufacturer in the US market at the time. More than 200,000 prefabricated houses were produced in the war years by more than 70 companies, some of them producing at a rate of 1,000 units a month. We will look at some of these other packaged houses in the next chapter. The mass-produced house was, and is, a perfectly feasible concept, especially in a time of housing crisis. Gilbert Herbert can never quite bring himself to say it out loud, but reading between the lines it is perfectly clear that the failure of the Packaged House should be blamed on one man, its inventor, Konrad Wachsmann. For Wachsmann the Packaged House was not really a house, not a locus for the lives of real people, not even 'a machine for living in'; it was an abstract geometrical system, tending always towards mathematical perfection. Wachsmann was obsessed with his system and could never stop 'improving' it, which meant making it conceptually as near perfect as he could. No sooner had one ingenious connector been patented than he had designed a better one. The system went through at least four redesigns before the factory was set up, and even as the production line was being installed Wachsmann exasperated his colleagues by deciding that the whole principle of the system was wrong and that the crucial four-way connector was in fact unnecessary. He could only be deflected from his obsession with the abstract system by involving him in the design of the production line, with the inevitable result that that too became an abstract system, a journey to an unreachable ideal. When production finally did get under way and it became obvious that the product was going to be too expensive, savings were made by simplifying the floor and roof elements, replacing the universal panels with ordinary joists and boards. This, says Herbert, caused Wachsmann 'great distress' because it compromised the universality of the system, which for him was all that really mattered.

Years later Wachsmann published another book, called *The Turning Point of Building*. In it he analyses various examples of industrialized building, from the Crystal Palace to his own space-frame hangar projects of the 1950s. 'In discarding many of our old ideas about building,' he says in the introduction, 'we have reached a turning point. The decisions about what constitutes the formative energies of the age have been made and the principles that will guide the developing forward movement are now apparent.'[8] What he means to say is that industrial production is on the point of transforming architecture and building. Twenty pages of *The Turning Point* are devoted to the Packaged House. Here we see more clearly Wachsmann's obsessive perfectionism. The text is mainly a minutely detailed, almost unreadable description of the dimensional logic of the system. For example:

> Although it must be generally assumed that the joint module is at least proportionally identical with the element module, it was nevertheless necessary to bear in mind that there are cases in which the element module, though dimensionally modified, is still to be brought into organic relationship with the joint module by means of addition or subtraction.[9]

The Burbank production line is also described and illustrated in great detail. But there is no mention of the fact that the project was a technical and commercial failure, only this rather evasive sentence:

> It had become possible to ship a whole house overnight from the factory to any site . . . and for that house to be erected on a previously prepared foundation by five unskilled workers in one day.[10]

It had become possible. It was enough for Wachsmann that the Packaged House had become possible. His satisfaction came not from the production of thousands of houses or the alleviation of a housing crisis, or even from the financial rewards that commercial success would bring; it came from the design of a perfect abstract system. When that system was as near complete as it could be, including the planning of the production line, his job was done. If the world didn't want it then it was the world, not the system, that was at fault. Herbert himself seems to support this view when he says, on the very last page of his book, that the proper conditions for the realization of the dream of the factory made house would have to include 'a society more amenable to logical discourse, rational decision making, and creative human interaction than we at present appear to be.' Wachsmann and Gropius, he says, are 'great men' and we must make allowances for them. But given that the Packaged House was one of dozens of prefabricated housing systems developed in the US in the 1940s and that most of the others were more successful, the question arises: why single it out for such close historical scrutiny? Why not write a book about, say, National Homes of Lafayette, Indiana, a company that quietly got on with producing about ten low-cost houses a day for which it found a ready market? To be fair to Herbert, he is well aware of the many rivals to the Packaged House and he details them meticulously in his footnotes. But this only makes it more puzzling that he should want to single out a project that had no impact on actual housing provision. The explanation is, of course, that this book is not about housing: it is about architecture. The story of the Packaged House is interesting not for what it tells us about American housing in the 1940s but for what it tells us about Gropius and Wachsmann. Strangely, Herbert does not see the failure of the Packaged House project as diminishing in any way the reputations of Gropius and Wachsmann as architects. Architects are judged by different standards. Their designs do not have to be successful in the worldly sense because they can be successful in an abstract sense as architecture. The houses produced by companies like National Homes *were* successful, but they were not designed by architects, so they don't count as architecture, and they don't become suitable subjects for architectural history.

Richard Buckminster Fuller was not, strictly speaking, an architect; he was a self-taught engineer and inventor. If we think of him as an architect it is because architectural history has awarded him that honorary title. He is perhaps most famous for the invention, or at least the patenting, of the geodesic dome, but earlier in his career his great dream had been to design a successful mass-produced house. The opportunity arose in 1944 when he was working for the Board of Economic Warfare in Washington. At that time aircraft factories were finding it difficult to retain their workers because of overcrowded temporary housing and a general scepticism about job prospects in the aircraft industry once the war was over. If the workers could be convinced that the factories were going to be converted to make peacetime products, then morale might be boosted and the labour force stabilized. And if those peacetime products were houses, then so much the better. Fuller's prefabricated house ideas were well known. Back in 1928 he had patented the Dymaxion House, a hexagonal metal house suspended by cables from a central mast. The project had received wide publicity, although no prototypes had ever been built. In 1936, while working for the Phelps Dodge Corporation, Fuller had designed the Dymaxion Bathroom, a forerunner of the prefabricated bathroom pod familiar now in hotel rooms all over the world. In 1940 he developed a low-cost portable house called the Dymaxion Deployment Unit (DDU), based on standard circular agricultural storage bins made by the Butler Manufacturing Company of Kansas. Thousands of DDUs had been ordered by the US Army for use as radar operating huts. Asked if he could produce a design for a prefabricated house to be manufactured in an aircraft factory, Fuller at first demurred on the basis that his designs were always 25 years ahead of their time and, since

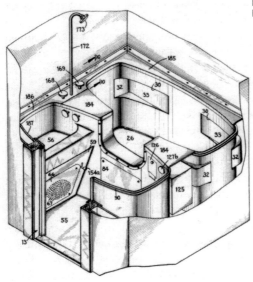

the Dymaxion House had been designed in 1927, it would not be ready for production until 1952. 'The time is premature', he said, 'for a consideration of this new industry as a commercially exploitable undertaking.'[11] In other words, the world was not yet ready for it. This initial hesitancy is important in the light of subsequent events. Before long, however, Fuller was presenting his ideas to Jack Gaty, the general manager of Beech Aircraft in Wichita, Kansas. What became known as the Wichita House would combine the three Dymaxion designs to create the most technically advanced individual family house the world had ever seen. Gaty agreed to allow Fuller free use of space on his production line, with the necessary tools and administrative support. A company was set up called Fuller Houses Inc., with Fuller as chief designer. Of course Gaty had an ulterior motive. He was more interested in preventing the leakage of his labour force than in manufacturing houses. And the ploy worked. The mere presence of the prototype production line and of Fuller himself, who made inspiring presentations to the workers, not only stemmed the flow of labour from the factory but actually reversed it. The Wichita House had, in a sense, already done its job without a single actual house being produced. But it was thought that a more permanent and visible sign of faith in the future was required and the US Army Air Corps was therefore persuaded to order two prototypes, giving them 'weapons priority'. Jack Gaty was happy to find room for one of them on the Beech factory site.

The Wichita House makes the Maison Citrohan and the Packaged House look like primitive huts. Though not as technically complex as an aeroplane it was nevertheless designed as if it were an aeroplane. Air flow was an important determinant of the form. The house's circular plan and shallow dome-like roof betrayed its grain bin parentage, but wind tunnel tests confirmed that the form was aerodynamically up to ten times more efficient than a rectangular house. Reducing wind resistance was important for the lateral stability of the structure but it also increased the energy efficiency of the house by reducing heat loss through the external envelope. The power of the wind was harnessed to increase ventilation by sucking air out through a big, keel-shaped rotating vent on top of the roof. Fuller thought of his house not as a static object but as a kind of vehicle – car, boat or plane – ploughing its way through the air at hurricane wind speeds. Air flow in the interior was also carefully controlled. Heating was by means of a 'fountain flow' of warm air from a central duct. The flow could be reversed for cooling. All mechanical, electrical and plumbing services, including two Dymaxion bathrooms, were grouped at the centre of the plan. The rest of the space was divided like a cake into five slices – living-room, two bedrooms, kitchen and entrance hall – by fat, radial partitions that contained revolving storage devices. But it was the structure that was really revolutionary. The whole house, including the profiled steel floor deck and an allowable live load of 120 people, was suspended from a central stainless-steel mast by a combination of criss-crossed tension cables and compression rings like the rims of bicycle wheels. Curved sheets of Duralumin, the same silvery, non-oxidizable alloy used to make Beech aircraft, covered the walls and roof, and the almost continuous horizontal ribbon window was made of 'plexiglass' with no opening lights. The house weighed only 6,000 lb (2,722 kg) and all the components could be packed onto a single truck. It was estimated that a team of six men could assemble it on site in one day.

The prototype was well received, crucially by the wives of Beech employees who might persuade their husbands to stay on at the factory, and as the war came to an end the Wichita House seemed poised to conquer the world. Beech declared that they could make 60,000 houses a year but a big article in *Fortune* magazine talked about a production rate of 250,000 a year. A very competitive retail price of $6,500 was quoted (about the same as a Cadillac) on the basis of limited mass production, but this figure, it was claimed, would come down to $3,700 in full mass production at a rate of 500,000 houses a year. The hype began to do its job and before long 3,700 purchase applications had been registered. (Historical accounts differ; some add a nought to this figure.)[12] But the factory was still not tooled up and this called for an investment of at least $10 million. It was proposed to raise this money by means of a share issue. At this

Model of the Wichita
House by Buckminster
Fuller.

Wichita House
salesman and
potential customer.

point, however, Fuller got cold feet, insisting that more development work was needed before the house could go into full production. Perhaps he just could not bear to see his 25-year development period law disproved, or perhaps he genuinely foresaw some ruinous technical disaster. He was, after all, in the best position to assess the feasibility of the project, whereas his colleagues had begun to believe their own publicity. Unfortunately for them, and for the workers at Beech, Fuller had retained a veto on all design issues when the company had been set up. There was nothing they could do. The delay lengthened, confidence ebbed away and eventually the company was liquidated. Only one house had been built.

In one sense the Wichita House project had been a success. It had made an important contribution to the war effort, improving morale in aircraft factories by offering the hope of peacetime employment. But very soon it became clear that the demand for armaments was not about to dry up and swords-to-ploughshares conversion projects were unnecessary. The Wichita House was as much the victim of the Cold War as of its designer's stubbornness and arrogance.

The Maison Citrohan, the Packaged House, the Wichita House: a pattern begins to emerge. The prefabricated houses that conventional architectural history chooses to canonize and celebrate, mainly because they were designed by famous architects, were all complete failures by any objective, non-architectural measure.

And these are not the only relevant cases. The prefabricated house is a recurring theme in the writings of Frank Lloyd Wright. In 1932 he gave a speech to a gathering of estate agents in which he described his idea for an 'Assembled House' made up of standard, room-size units.[13] Customers would buy the basic minimum of three units – bathroom, kitchen and one bedroom – and add more rooms when they were needed. Standardized kitchens and what would now be called bathroom pods were already available on the market (Buckminster Fuller's Dymaxion bathroom was not patented until 1938, but less sophisticated versions by other inventors had been patented as early as 1931) and other rooms would be made from insulated metal panels. There would be several possible unit configurations to suit site conditions and customer requirements. 'The design of these things in the first place can be of such a character that in the final assembly no wrong or bad thing can happen', said Wright, with typical confidence, dismissing the whole problem of dimensional co-ordination in an airy phrase. Six years later, in an article for the Chicago magazine *Inland Topics*, Wright returns to the theme of prefabrication, but this time warning that in the wrong hands – those of 'superficial speculators' and 'stylists' – the factory built house would lack 'artistic integrity': '[The prefabricated house] must be no makeshift but must be radical architecture in an organic sense as not only a good machine is but also as any natural thing is. Say, a tree.'[14]

Wright didn't just theorize about prefabrication; he designed and built several prefabricated houses using a variety of technologies. As early as 1916 he had designed a 'Ready-Cut' prefabrication system for individual houses and duplex flats. Essentially it was an adaptation of conventional American 'balloon frame' construction, but with every joist, plate, stud, beam and rafter cut to the required length in the factory, marked, packed and delivered to the site as a kit. A few small developments were built in Milwaukee and at least one survives to this day, but the system was soon abandoned. In 1937 Wright designed an all-steel prefabrication system for housing in Los Angeles but failed to find a sponsor.[15] In 1956 the Marshall Erdman Company of Madison, Wisconsin, began to manufacture and market prefabricated houses to Wright's designs. 'Frank Lloyd Wright has at long last built a prefab house', began a detailed article in the magazine *House and Home*. 'It is big news', the article went on, 'because it gives prefabrication – once the stepchild of home building – the prestige associated with the greatest name in contemporary architecture.'[16] Prestige, however, was not enough to guarantee commercial success. Construction was actually fairly conventional, combining timber-framed masonite wall panels with ordinary concrete blockwork, but the houses were still too expensive and only about twenty were actually delivered and built.

Of all Wright's attempts to design moderately priced houses for ordinary people, it is the so-called Usonian Houses of the late 1930s and '40s that history remembers best. Usonia was Wright's name for the USA, but an imagined USA, a USA designed by Frank Lloyd Wright. The Usonian House was meant to be a house suitable for the average American family. In practice, this meant the average American middle-class family. The Usonian houses were modest by the standards of Wright's earlier Prairie Houses, but their clients tended to be journalists, academics and business executives rather than factory workers. And Wright's relationships with his clients were almost always on a personal, or pseudo-personal, level. He would, for example, often invite them to stay for weekends at Taliesin, his headquarters in Wisconsin, perhaps to make sure they were not going to become too difficult or demanding. The clients, for their part, were flattered by the attentions of the great man and found themselves willing to accept his suggestions. After all, the most important feature of their house would always be that it had been designed by Frank Lloyd Wright. When a famous architect designs a house, the client necessarily becomes a patron rather than a customer.

The Usonian houses were not standardized or mass-produced, but neither were they entirely one-offs. Of course, every architect carries over tried and tested details from job to job and no building is invented completely from scratch, but in the Usonian houses this *ad hoc* continuity became a thoroughgoing system. The most important manifestation of the system was a controlling 4 by 2 ft (1200 by 600 mm) planning grid, like the 6 by 3 ft (1800 by 900 mm) Tatami mat grid of the traditional Japanese house that had been such a powerful influence on Wright early in his career. And like the Japanese house, the Usonian house was also governed by a standard vertical grid, worked out to conform to both brick courses and standard milled (planed) timber sizes. The standard grid simplified planning and setting out, and a book of standard details simplified construction. Normally single-storey, the house had no basement and no deep foundations, just a thin concrete ground-bearing slab. Walls were made of plywood sandwiched between horizontal cypress boards. Windows mostly took the form of long stretches of full-height glazing, incorporating glass doors. All roofs were flat, usually at two levels with clerestory windows in between, and with generous overhangs.

This is the kind of systematization that one associates with factory production. It would surely have been easy to have prefabricated the wall and roof panels in standard sizes, drawn up a family of house plans, marketed the product under the Frank Lloyd Wright brand name and transformed the look of suburban America. As we have seen, it wasn't really that easy, but then Wright never seems to have considered this possibility seriously anyway. As he saw it, the balance between factory production and site assembly was already optimized. The factory-made components were mainly bricks, milled timber and joinery items such as windows, doors and built-in furniture. Site work was minimized not by prefabrication but by rationalization of the design. There were no wet finishes, no plaster or paint, just naked wood and brickwork, and, instead of the usual central heating system, the Usonian houses used underfloor heating, an innovation at the time. This was fairly easy to install, but more importantly it simplified the construction sequence and the detailing of the interior by eliminating radiators.

The classic Usonian house is the Jacobs house of Madison, Wisconsin, built for a young journalist and his wife. It has a relaxed, indeterminate plan, basically L-shaped, with a service core of kitchen and bathroom at the intersection of the bedroom and living-room wings. Placed on the corner of the site, it embraces the garden rather than sitting within it. The kitchen is a kind of control centre, open to the main circulation route between living-room and bedroom corridor so that the wife (this is 1938) can easily supervise the children. But a straightforward description cannot really do justice to the house. The

Interior of the Jacobs House by Frank Lloyd Wright.

main thing to say is that, for all its modesty and simplicity, it effortlessly and unquestionably achieves the status of 'architecture'. One only has to compare it to Gropius and Wachsmann's clever but curiously rigid building system, or Fuller's glorified grain bin, or even Le Corbusier's confused Purist vernacular, to appreciate Wright's artistry. Roofs hover and overlap; walls define and stabilize; light falls just so; space flows. The American suburban house would never be the same again. Unlike Le Corbusier, whose architecture was only ever appreciated by an élite minority, Frank Lloyd Wright was attuned to popular taste. His name was known and his houses were regularly featured in lifestyle and women's magazines, not to mention *Time* and *Life*. And unlike Le Corbusier's urban vision of communal apartment blocks standing in parkland, Frank Lloyd Wright's city of the future – he called it Broadacre City – was dispersed, low rise and individualistic: a plot of land, a detached house and a car for every family. This is the environment that the average American prefers to live in and Frank Lloyd Wright played his part in its eventual triumph. Perhaps the most important innovation of the Usonian House, both spatially and culturally, was its carport.

The extent of Wright's influence is arguable, but one thing is definite: very few Usonian houses were actually built. The picture is confused because Wright attached the name 'Usonian' to almost every house he designed after

1938, but the generally agreed figure for the true Usonians is about 26. By no stretch of the imagination can this be described as mass-production. Wright was used to the traditional architect-client relationship and it served his purposes very well, but he could not afford to squander his artistry on every $5,000 house. He needed a system, a kind of shorthand that would allow him to design quickly and delegate the details to an apprentice. (Wright insisted that the client should house and feed the apprentice during the whole construction period, this on top of a flat 10 per cent fee.) The system was not foolproof but it reduced 'on costs' (the cost of design) and it produced beautiful houses. Its potential for industrial production, however, was never realized. The architects of the other houses discussed in this chapter were trying to design for mass production, whereas Wright was simply trying to rationalize his one-off houses. The irony is that of them all the Usonian was probably the house with the most mass-market potential.

One more would-be mass-production house of the mid-twentieth century has edged its way into architectural history, though its designer, like Buckminster Fuller, was not strictly speaking an architect. Jean Prouvé is known now chiefly as a designer of structural frames and cladding systems but he began his career in 1918 as an art metalworker with a small workshop in Nancy, France. By the mid-1920s, in collaboration with well-known architects such as Robert Mallet Stevens and Tony Garnier, he was designing and making architectural fittings and furniture using advanced techniques like electric welding and structural folded steel. In 1935 he designed a small, all-metal weekend house with the architects Beaudouin and Lods. It was intended for mass-production but never got beyond the prototype – a light, portable building that suffered an unusual fate: it was stolen in 1939. From the outbreak of war to the German occupation, Prouvé's workshop (which at this time employed Le Corbusier's cousin, Pierre Jeanneret) produced emergency accommodation, including prefabricated 3 by 3 metre huts to house soldiers. Each hut could be erected by three men in one hour. After the liberation the Minister of Reconstruction ordered 800 temporary houses for the homeless based on the same principles as the soldiers' huts. Photographs of these houses under construction show an unusual combination of folded steel frame and load-bearing timber panels. The appearance of the finished houses was somewhere between the utilitarian and the downright agricultural. At this point the historical record becomes rather hazy.[17] We know that 800 of these houses were ordered and that various buildability tests were carried out on the prototype, but there is some doubt as to how many were actually built. As late as 1985, however, it was claimed that some still existed and were in good condition.[18]

Meudon House by Jean Prouvé.

In 1949 Eugene Claudius-Petit, friend and patron of Le Corbusier, became the new Minister for Reconstruction. As part of his effort to improve the French government's appalling record in housing provision since the war, he ordered 25 experimental, prefabricated but permanent and well-appointed houses from the Prouvé workshop. The houses were to cost no more than the cheapest conventional equivalents. Prouvé complained that this was an unreasonable restriction because the order was too small to justify the necessary investment. Nevertheless, he went ahead and produced all the necessary components. Here once again the historical record becomes suspiciously vague.[19] Apparently no delivery instructions were issued and the houses took up valuable space in the workshop for a year or more until an exasperated Prouvé invited his workers, themselves badly housed, to help themselves to them. Eventually, however, instructions did arrive from the ministry to erect some of the remaining houses in a park in the Paris suburb of Meudon, where they remain, thoroughly gentrified, to this day. They have come to be known simply as 'The Meudon Houses' and now have a secure place in the canon of architectural history, but they were never tested or appraised and the experiment was abandoned.

In the early 1950s the Prouvé workshop employed about 200 people producing furniture, architectural components and prefabricated buildings at a semi-industrial rate. A few years earlier the enterprise had received an injection of capital from L'Aluminium Français and the parent company, seeking a bigger return on its investment, now began to interfere with what had previously been Prouvé's exclusive domain. In 1953 he was ousted from his own workshop and set up a consultancy business in Paris, breaking the direct connection with production that he had always considered essential to good design.

With the possible exception of Frank Lloyd Wright's Usonians, all of the above houses, taken from that narrow and selective view of the past that we call architectural history, were designed with the serious intention of putting them into mass-production. In the second half of the twentieth century, however, the relationship between architecture and the mass-produced house changed. Architects – or at least the sort of architects that history celebrates – seemed to lose the will to change the world by direct intervention and instead put their faith in influence and example. There is no shortage of architect-designed houses that could be mass-produced, houses that embody ideas about mass production, or houses that simply look mass-produced. But they are mostly one-off demonstration pieces, designed in offices and studios by architects who have no real desire to subject themselves to the discipline of the factory. Most famous of these is the Eames House in Pacific Palisades, California, designed in 1949 for their own use by the architect Charles Eames and his artist

The Eames House.

wife Ray. The house was quite explicitly a demonstration piece, one of a series of 'Case Study Houses' commissioned from various architects by John Entenza, the editor of *Arts and Architecture* magazine. Several of them – 1635 Woods Drive, Los Angeles, by Pierre Koenig, for example – have found their niche in architectural history with the assistance of the photographer Julius Shulman, whose images of the casual Californian lifestyle are what the coffee-table book was invented for.

Most case study houses are single-storey, flat-roofed, open-plan, and timber- or steel-framed, with glass walls sliding open onto poolside patios. The Eames House, though, is different: a pair of two-storey boxes, one for the house and one for the studio, steel-framed and clad not in big sheets of plate glass but in ordinary steel window sashes straight from the manufacturer's catalogue. Areas of solid infill are painted in bright colours so that the elevations look like paintings by Mondrian. The steel frame is also assembled from standard catalogue components. Lattice joists and the profiled metal roof deck that they support, are left exposed internally, as they might be in a cheap industrial building. An earlier scheme for the house was completely different: a single-storey bridge structure, fully glazed and rather too obviously influenced by that other great German emigré form-giver, Mies van der Rohe. It might have been Ray who persuaded Charles to rethink the design and avoid the Miesian cliché. She later claimed that the new design had reused the steel that had already been delivered to build the first design. This can't be true (the dimensions simply don't add up), but it reinforces the idea of the house as an assemblage of mass-produced components that might one day be disassembled and rearranged.[20] Extravagant claims were also made for the cheapness and speed of erection of the house. They are not true either (they fail to take into account the availability of free student labour and the time it took to fit out the interior), but in a demonstration house the idea matters more than the reality.

The Eameses never developed their catalogue component house idea and soon abandoned architecture altogether in favour of a new kind of practice, combining furniture, exhibition and industrial design with film-making. The house was, however, enormously influential among architects, especially British architects like their friends and admirers, Alison and Peter Smithson. Britain provides some of the best examples of what might be called the one-off mass-produced house. In the late 1960s those grand old men of British architecture, Richard Rogers and Norman Foster, were briefly in partnership together. They initiated a new style that came to be known as British High Tech, developing it in ever-bigger projects over the next twenty years. High Tech architects loved the idea of factory-produced components in metal or plastic that could be rapidly assembled on site without all the mess and inaccuracy of concrete or brick or wood. Individual houses were not their speciality; they were better at factories and office buildings on greenfield sites, like Reliance Controls in Swindon (1967), which is generally acknowledged as the first true High Tech building. But Buckminster Fuller, Jean Prouvé and the Eameses were their heroes, so it was natural that when they did come to design a house, usually for themselves or for a sympathetic relative, they should approach it as if it were a prototype for-mass production.

In 1968 the chemical company Dupont, which made neoprene gaskets among other things, sponsored a design competition called House for Today. Nobody remembers who won it, but Richard Rogers came second with the Zip-up House, a kind of Yellow Submarine on legs; pink legs. Highly insulated aluminium sandwich panels joined by neoprene gaskets were formed into a structural rectangular tube with rounded corners. It was glazed at the ends and punctured by bus windows, and the space inside could be divided up as the user pleased by mobile partitions locked into position pneumatically. The spindly steel legs were adjustable to accommodate sloping sites. Perhaps harder to build than it looked, it was nevertheless a beautifully simple concept and an appealing image (especially to architecture students). In the same year, Rogers designed and built a less technically advanced version, with a steel frame and without the legs, for his mother in Wimbledon.

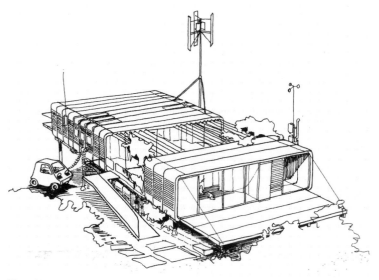

Zip-up House by Richard Rogers.

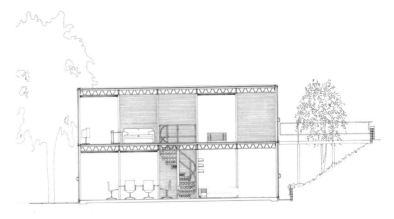

Hopkins House by Michael Hopkins.

In 1975 Michael Hopkins, an ex-partner of Norman Foster, and his wife, Patty, built themselves a version of the Eames house in Hampstead. The small, horizontal glazing divisions had gone, as had the coloured infill panels, but the inspiration for the lattice trusses, the profiled metal decking and the exposed cross-bracing was never in doubt. It may not have been assembled from catalogue components, but it looked as if it had been: a simple project for Meccano set number one. Nothing much had changed since 1949, except that some of the joy had drained away. It was the 1970s equivalent not of the Eames house as built, but of the Mies-inspired precursor that Ray rejected.

The final High Tech example is by another offspring of the Foster office, Richard Horden, who in 1984 built a house for a relative in the New Forest. Called the Yacht House, it was an example of 'technology transfer', a favourite High Tech theme. The particular piece of technology being transferred in this case was a tubular aluminium yacht mast. This component was used to construct a single-storey 'wind frame' acting as an armature for a family of roof, wall and screen panels. Like the Hopkins house, the Yacht House was a simple assemblage of a few standard components.

These High Tech houses were, in a sense, specifically designed to be mass-produced. Mass production is what, architecturally, they are 'about'. But their designers never seriously contemplated taking the steps necessary to begin production: identifying collaborators and investors, finding premises, producing business plans, launching marketing campaigns, planning production lines. Le Corbusier, Gropius, Wachsmann, Fuller, Prouvé, even Wright *did* seriously contemplate these things. Their various enterprises all failed in commercial terms, but they still saw themselves, and were seen by their industrial partners, as part

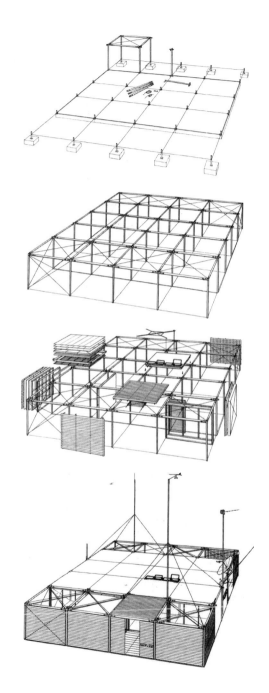

Yacht House by Richard
Horden. Assembly
sequence.

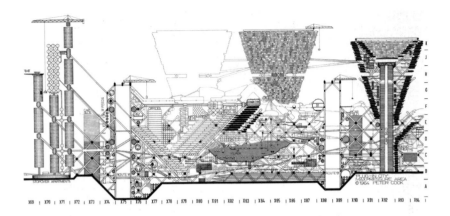

Plug in City drawing by Archigram.

of the production process. Since the 1950s architects have retreated from this position, distancing themselves from the factory even when their architecture pays lip service to its disciplines. 'Factory produced' has become a style, and a style of very limited appeal outside the architectural field. If any of these houses were to be subjected to the disciplines of the factory and the market they would certainly change, probably quite radically. Would their architects then disown them? And would they therefore cease to be architecture?

But at least the High Tech prototype houses are real buildings. The precursor of the High Tech style was a collection of paper projects produced throughout the 1960s by a group of architects called Archigram, after the magazine (*Archi*tecture tele*gram*) that they produced.[21] Three members of the group, Ron Herron, Warren Chalk and Dennis Crompton, worked in the architects department of London County Council, where they designed the infamous South Bank arts complex, an important example of the style known as 'Brutalism'. The other three members, Peter Cook, David Greene and Mike Webb, then fairly recent graduates, worked for the construction company Taylor Woodrow, but were eventually destined for academic careers. Though some resemblance is discernible between the South Bank complex and certain early Archigram projects, generally speaking concrete monuments were anathema to Archigram. They visualized a dynamic, flexible, indeterminate, throwaway alternative to what by then had become the old-fashioned modernism of Corb and Gropius. But the mass-produced dwelling was still an important theme. It was Archigram that first began to use words like 'capsule' and 'pod' rather than 'house' or 'home'. One the best-known projects, Plug-in-City, envisaged an enormous megastructure of diagonal steel tubes, 2.75 metres

Living Pod model by Archigram.

(9 ft) thick and spanning 44 metres (144 ft), to which thousands of living pods clung like barnacles, in some places forming funnel-shaped towers around car silos a hundred storeys high. Note the strange combination of realism and fantasy: the worked-out dimensions of the structure; the vertiginous nightmare of the environment it creates. In hindsight, we seem to be in *Blade Runner* territory, but this was meant to be a consumer playground, not a dystopian warning.

At closer range and in smaller numbers, the pods and capsules looked more believable. In Warren Chalk's 1964 Capsule Homes project, for example, identical mass-produced units were straightforwardly attached to a concrete core to make an almost ordinary-looking tower block. In Japan at this time, Kisho Kurokawa, a member of the Metabolist group, was developing similar designs, and in 1972 he actually built one, the famous Nagakin Capsule Tower in Tokyo. David Greene's Living Pod of 1966 looked like a stomach on lunar module legs (although this was three years before the first lunar landing). It had a 'transparent entry seal' instead of a front door, 'wash capsules' instead of bathrooms and a 'clothing dispenser' instead of a wardrobe, but it wouldn't have looked out of place on the more relaxed kind of American trailer park. Archigram were

# THERE IS A GAP
## BETWEEN IDEA AND IMAGE

left: EXPANDING HOUSE
by CESARE PEA
below: BATHROOM
(patent drawing) by
BUCKMINSTER FULLER

THE NEAREST THE BRITISH PUBLIC IS ALLOWED TO GET TO HAVING EXPENDABLE BUILDINGS
THAT ARE WHAT THEY ARE - UNASHAMEDLY - CHALETS. HUTS. CARAVANS - ALL HAVE FAILED

SOME... FORM...

PROBLEM : IS THIS EXPENDABLE ARCHITECTURE ?

SOME THINGS BRIDGE THE GAP

'There is a gap…' – page from *Archigram* magazine issue 3.

conscious of the potentially embarrassing fact that many of their futuristic inventions already existed in places like seaside resorts, oil exploration rigs and suburban back gardens. A collaged page in *Archigram* 3, devoted to 'expendability', expresses this unease. 'There is a gap between idea and image', says the caption, 'some things bridge the gap' (images of architecturally respectable artefacts like Buckminster Fuller's Dymaxion Bathroom), 'some things don't' (cutaway drawings of caravans and a page from a garden shed catalogue). The message is clear: it is image that matters. Another caption on the 'damned' side of the page reads: 'The nearest the British Public is allowed to get to having expendable buildings that are what they are – chalets, huts, caravans – all have failed.' Plainly the opposite was true. These things had failed only in Archigram terms. In every other way, they had succeeded. That was why they were in the collage.[22]

In the early 1970s the Archigram group tried to set up a proper architectural practice, but it did not last long and it built virtually nothing. Archigram's place in history, however, is secure. The images endure because architects have found them inspiring. As Martin Pawley has pointed out, Archigram 'failed in every market place except the art gallery'.[23] And for the architectural establishment of the new century, success in the art gallery is enough to warrant the highest honour. In 2001 Archigram was awarded the Royal Institute of British Architects' Gold Medal.

# 2. A non-architectural history

The houses described in the previous chapter are all well known to architects. Together they constitute a selective but nevertheless tolerably representative architectural history of the prefabricated house. Many more examples might have been included: Mies van der Rohe's Court-Houses of the 1930s, Albert Frey's Aluminaire House, Richard Neutra's Diatom House, Alison and Peter Smithson's House of the Future. But it would have made no difference. The awful truth is that as industrial products these houses were all either failures or non-starters. There are architectural lessons to be learnt from them – about domestic and industrial space, about individual and collective form, about the surprising closeness of the factory-made and the vernacular – but one thing you can't learn from them, except in a negative sense, is how to make cheap, practical houses that ordinary people want to buy or rent. This doesn't mean that the prefabricated house has been a failure. There are plenty of examples of successful prefabricated houses. It is just that they have not been canonized by architectural history. It sometimes seems that commercial and industrial success is itself sufficient to disqualify a prefabricated house from the status of architecture.

The non-architectural history of the prefabricated house begins a little earlier than its better-known counterpart. It was in 1833 in Chicago that the 'balloon frame' was invented. It was to become, and still is, the basic technology of popular housing in America, Northern Europe (though not Britain), Australia and Japan. What exactly is a balloon frame? Foundations and roofs of balloon frame houses vary. It is the walls and floors that are characteristic. Typically, the walls are formed by vertical timber 'studs', usually 2 by 4 in (50 by 100 mm) in cross section, spaced 16 in (400 mm) apart and nailed to horizontal 'plates' top and bottom. In a two-storey house, the studs extend over the full height, with a 'ribbon' let into them on the inside, halfway up, to support the joists or beams of the upper floor. When the framing is finished, the whole structure is covered with 'siding', traditionally of overlapping wooden 'clapboards' nailed to the studs.

It took a hundred years for architectural history to register the birth of the balloon frame, in an essay called 'American Development in Design' by Sigfried Giedion, published in 1939 in *New Directions*.[1] Most architects first read about it, however, in Giedion's great textbook of Modernism, *Space, Time and Architecture*, first published in 1941 and still to be found on architectural students' reading lists.[2] So immediately it seems our non-architectural history is indebted to an architectural historian. Giedion did not, however, see the balloon frame house as a piece of architecture in its own right. He was interested in it only as an example of the industrial and economic forces that eventually gave rise to his real subject, the Modernist architecture of the twentieth century.

Even when writing the history of non-architecture, an architectural historian needs to know the names of the authors of designs, and Giedion was therefore obliged to name the inventor of the balloon frame. He settled on one George W. Snow. Snow was born in New Hampshire in 1797 and first arrived in Chicago on 12 July 1832, 'in a canoe paddled by an Indian guide' (the mystique of author-ship depends on little details like this). Snow had been trained as a civil engineer and was soon appointed Chicago's first assessor and surveyor. By 1835 he had bought a lumber yard and was running a successful real estate business. In 1849 he was elected alderman. A portrait photograph in a family album reveals, Giedion tells us, 'a face at once full of puritan energy and of human sensitivity'. Unfortunately, these interesting personal details and colourful speculations are

Erection of an unusually large balloon frame structure.

probably irrelevant, because later research by Walker Field indicates that it was not Snow, but a carpenter by the name of Augustine Deodat Taylor who invented the balloon frame.[3] Field and Giedion, however, do at least agree on one thing: that the first true balloon frame building was not a house but a church, St Mary's, on Lake Street, built by Taylor between July and October 1833 for Father John M. I. St Cyr and his congregation.

Chicago was a boom town. The population in 1833 was 350; five years later it would be 4,000, and by 1850, 30,000. Land to the west had been cleared of its rightful owners by the Black Hawk War, and white settlers poured into the town to stake their claims, living in their covered wagons because of the shortage of lodgings. Buildings were needed fast but there were very few skilled craftsmen available and the old post-and-beam method of construction, using hefty, hand-finished timbers and traditional carpentry joints, could not keep pace with demand. Fortunately, industrial production provided two new 'raw' materials: accurately sawn timber and mass-produced nails.

The first steam-driven saw had been patented in 1793. Steam power tended to encourage standardization of timber sizes because it could drive multiple, evenly spaced saws. By 1832 Chicago had its own steam saw mill, although it seems to have produced only relatively crude planks. In 1833, however, David Carver, 'the founder of Chicago lumbering', began importing sawn timber from St Joseph in his schooner. By 1839 Chicago had become a timber distribution centre for the Midwest. In the colonial era, nail making, a laborious hand forging process, had been one of the 'secondary manufactures' expressly forbidden by the British, who looked upon the colony as a captive market for such products. From 1790 onwards, however, several patents were registered for nail-making machines and in 1807 Jesse Reed invented a machine that could produce 60,000 good-quality nails in a day. Accurately sawn timber and mass-produced nails were the true begetters of the balloon frame.

When Augustine Taylor bravely abandoned tradition and decided to use nails to fix the slender frame of the new church on Lake Street, onlookers were sceptical. It was too light, they said, and it would blow away like a balloon in the first gale. The balloon gibe stuck, but they were wrong. The building proved very durable, so durable that in its long life it was twice dismantled and re-erected on new sites. Very soon every Chicago builder was nailing up balloon frames. They were fast, they were cheap and they were just what the town needed. 150 houses were erected in the spring and summer of 1834 alone. Just one week became the accepted period of construction for a simple shack. Within ten years Chicago had become balloon frame city and the technique had become the standard method of construction right across the frontier. Its potential for prefabrication was quickly realized. In 1872 Horace Greely wrote:

Balloon frame drugstore, St Augustine, Florida.

> With the application of machinery, the labor of house building has been greatly lessened, and the western prairies are dotted over with houses which have been shipped there all made, and the various pieces numbered, so that they could be put up complete by anyone.[4]

The resulting small town architecture was lovingly recreated on the sets of Hollywood westerns.

While the balloon frame house was staking out the first cities of the American West, in Britain a true prefabricated house was being developed to meet the needs of war and colonization. British colonists and prospectors setting out for Australia or South Africa in the early nineteenth century faced a special kind of accommodation problem. When they arrived in the colony they would have to live in tents, suffering the heat, the dust and the storms, and more importantly the attentions of pilfering natives (or shipmates), until they could get themselves well enough organized to build a house from whatever unfamiliar materials happened to be lying around. If the ship's carpenter had departed, the house would have to be built without any skilled help. The answer, for those who could afford it, was to have a demountable house delivered ready packed to the dockside in England, stow it in the hold of the ship and travel with it. In 1830, John Manning, a London builder, published a brochure in which he advertised just such a house, hoping to sell it to emigrants to the Swan River Colony in Western Australia. The house, said the advertisement, could be 'erected in a few hours after landing, with windows, glazed doors, and locks, bolts, and the whole painted in a good and secure manner'.

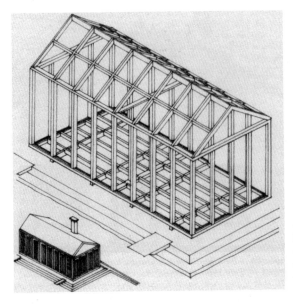

Drawing of a
Manning Portable
Cottage from an
advertisement in the
*South Australian
Record*, 1837.

It was so successful that within a few years the 'Manning Cottage', like Nissen
Hut and Portakabin a hundred or more years later, had entered the colonist's
everyday vocabulary. Soon there were competitors, but none could match the
sturdy practicality of the original. It was a simple box with a double pitched
roof and a wooden post-and-beam frame, pre-cut and bolted together on site.
The posts, spaced three feet apart, were grooved to receive a range of standard,
storey-height wall, door and window panels. The roof, the least sturdy element,
was of canvas. No special skill was required to assemble the house and, since
none of the components was too big to be carried by one man, it could just as
easily be disassembled and moved to another site. It cost £15.[5]

Manning had used the phrase 'portable colonial cottage' to define his product and this designation was adopted by his competitors and followers. The
wooden post-and-beam structure, however, was soon superseded by a new
technology and a new material: corrugated iron. In 1844 Thomas Edington
and Sons of Glasgow patented a rolling process for the volume production of
curved and flat corrugated iron sheets. Strong, light, durable, waterproof and
cheap, corrugated iron was the answer to a prefabricator's dream, especially
when galvanized (coated with zinc) to prevent corrosion. A complete self-
supporting roof could be made from a single curved sheet just a couple of mil-
limetres thick – a form that was to be used for cheap industrial and agricultural
buildings for the next hundred years.

Even in the 1840s and '50s corrugated iron was considered an unsympathetic material in a domestic setting, but fastidiousness was quickly overcome in emergencies like the California gold rush. San Francisco in 1849 was full of rich, homeless people. Every inch of accommodation was let, prices were sky high and conditions were sordid. The local building industry was virtually non-existent so prefabrication was the obvious answer. Entrepreneurs in New York, Philadelphia and Baltimore were quick to respond, making full use of the latest technology imported from England. It is estimated that about 5,000 prefabricated houses were shipped from New York alone in the first half of 1849, some sailing all the way round the Horn, others being carried by pack mule over the Panama isthmus. Peter Naylor, a roofer of Stone Street, New York, became the biggest manufacturer, shipping more than 500 house kits of English corrugated iron. His advertisement in the *Journal of Commerce* claimed that a complete house could be packed into two boxes, each 12 ft by 2 ft by 8 in, 'the freight on which would be about $14 to San Francisco'. A Naylor house purchased in New York for $345 could be sold in California for $5,000.[6]

Throughout the 1850s manufacturers such as Edward Bellhouse of Manchester, Charles Young of Glasgow, John Walker of Bermondsey and Samuel Hemming of Bristol produced prefabricated iron houses by the thousand for the Californian, Australian, South African and South American markets. It is hard to be precise about the volume, but Gilbert Herbert (who is once again the chief authority) cites a contemporary report of 1854 indicating that 30,329 'packages' of iron houses were imported into the state of Victoria in that year alone.[7] A number of different structural systems were used. Samuel Hemming used a frame of either wood or wrought iron, sheathed in corrugated iron externally and lined with wooden boards internally. Edward Bellhouse combined corrugated iron with another advanced material: cast iron. In 1853 he patented a system with round cast-iron columns flanged to receive panels of corrugated iron spanning horizontally between them.

After 1860 the portable cottage business declined as the colonies began to develop their own building industries and as the technical shortcomings of corrugated iron, particularly its low thermal mass, which made the houses unbearably hot in sub-tropical climates, assumed greater importance. But the portable cottage is only a small part of the history of prefabrication in the nineteenth century. Houses, hospitals, hotels, barracks, cotton factories, corn mills, ironworks, warehouses, markets, custom houses, clubhouses, pubs, theatres, railway stations, lock-keepers' cottages, palaces for African kings (King Eyambo of Nigeria ordered a Palladian palace of corrugated iron from Laycock of Liverpool in 1843) – all were prefabricated in iron or wood, mostly to be sent overseas. This is not to mention the urban warehouse and office façades made

Iron mission room made by Boulton and Paul in 1886 for Hendon in Oxfordshire, re-erected at the Chiltern Open Air Museum.

Iron mission room interior.

from elaborate kits of cast-iron components by companies like Walter Macfarlane and Co. of Glasgow and James Bogardus of New York. Then there were the churches. Even this most honorific, and most architectural, of building types was subject to the logic of prefabrication. With a few exceptions, like Matthew Digby Wyatt, who was commissioned by the East India Company to design a corrugated iron church for export to Rangoon, architects either ignored or despised iron churches. But manufacturers went ahead and produced their own designs, publishing them in pattern books in a range of styles and sizes. Corrugated iron churches and chapels became a common sight in London and Manchester as much as in Melbourne and Johannesburg.

Buying a house from a mail order catalogue seems like no more than an amusing fantasy but it was common practice in the us in the early years of the twentieth century. After the almost universal adoption of the balloon frame method of timber construction and pattern book designs (see Chapter 5), the next logical step was to send the customer not just the plans for a house but all the materials and components necessary to build it. Several companies offered mail order houses but the biggest and most famous was Sears Roebuck of Newark, New Jersey. The Sears spring catalogue of 1908 included four pages of houses, but there was also a separate house catalogue offering 22 different models at prices ranging from $650 to $2,500. 'Our plans', said the blurb, 'are more complete and simple than you can get from ordinary architects.'[8] The houses sold well and soon Sears were offering customers advantageous finance deals to help pay for the site and the labour as well as the house itself. Occasionally, bulk orders were received: in 1919 Standard Oil built a whole company town from Sears houses at Carlinville, Illinois. By 1925 ten sales offices had been set up in north-eastern and midwestern cities. Five years later the sales-force had risen to 350, based in 48 offices. Most customers now discussed their purchase with a salesperson or a sales team. There were many important decisions to be made: which house type, how it should be customized, how much Sears Roebuck furniture to buy with it, and whether to take advantage of the site supervision service.

A Sears Roebuck house kit was essentially a big bundle of timber, pre-cut and letter-keyed to framing plans at a scale of three-eighths of an inch to a foot (1:32), plus all the necessary secondary components like windows, doors, siding and shingles. Nails and paint were supplied, but not bricks or concrete. Plumbing, heating, wiring and an early version of drywall lining were optional. Houses were always delivered by rail, typically in two boxcars each. Sears claimed that buying a house in kit form saved about 40 per cent of labour costs and resulted in higher-quality construction owing to the improved accuracy of

# Our Honor Bilt Ready Cut System
## The Sure Way to Reduce Building Costs

Pieces numbered to correspond with plans.

Doors mortised for locks.

Note the notches and miters. No use for a saw here.

Every piece cut to fit.

A most difficult job made easy.

All sets of window and door trim of this design are cut to exact size. No sawing required. Head trim already nailed together.

Page from a Sears Roebuck house catalogue of 1926.

machine-cut timber. This is what the 1937 catalogue had to say about the company's main factory in Cairo, Illinois: 'This is the age of modern efficiency. No longer can human hands compete with machine precision and production. Speed with accuracy is the watchword in any department of our great factory.'[9] Four hundred and fifty different Sears Roebuck house types have been identified. None is attributed to a named architect, although there was an 'architectural division' under the leadership of David S. Betcone, and a Miss E. L. Meyer was for a time responsible for interior design. Sears Roebuck's pattern book was no different in this respect from dozens of others. House design in the US has always been cheap and plentiful. The depression hit Sears Roebuck's Modern Homes Department hard, particularly its mortgage section. It was closed down in 1934 but revived the following year to sell houses manufactured by General Houses Inc., without mortgages, but in 1940 Sears Roebuck finally pulled out of housing for good.

The mention of General Houses Inc. introduces another episode in the history of the American prefabricated house. Sears Roebuck never claimed to make any contribution to the progress of modern architecture. Its houses were indistinguishable from their ordinary, site-built neighbours and its pattern books included all the popular traditional styles, such as Craftsman, Colonial and Victorian. General Houses, however, at least in the early stages of its development, took the view that prefabricated houses ought to look modern. As sophisticated products of modern industry they had no business adopting pre-industrial forms. The man behind this idea was, not surprisingly, an architect, Howard T. Fisher , Harvard-trained and well-connected. In 1932 he founded General Houses with the support of prominent industrialists, including Owen D. Young, the president of General Electric, and Charles A. Liddle, president of Pullman Cars. This was a period when big business was taking an interest in prefabricated housing as a possible new growth area for investment and employment, the means by which the country might build its way out of the Depression. Fisher's idea, as the company's name implied, was to make houses the way General Motors made cars. It would be an enterprise based not on production but on co-ordination, or what we would now call 'supply chain management'. Different companies would make different components according to General Houses's specification and deliver them straight to the building site. Pullman, for example, would supply steel panels and Curtis Companies Inc. would supply the joinery. Fisher had already built a single-storey prototype for the dancer Ruth Page (his sister-in-law), and its well-proportioned, flat-roofed form, with square windows arranged in ribbons, made his modernist ambitions clear. Two demonstration houses were built in 1933 and 1934 at the Chicago Century of Progress exhibition.

They differed slightly in construction, but both had walls of interchangeable load-bearing steel panels, storey-height and 4 ft (1200 mm) wide, with a flush outer face and a 'pan' profile to take a filling of insulation. When the company set about selling its product to a mass market, however, both the technology and the architecture began to change. The load-bearing panel system was first replaced by a more conventional steel frame infilled with plywood-lined panels of asbestos-cement, and then by ordinary timber frame and siding. According to H. Ward Jandl's account, 'several hundred' of General Houses's 'modern looking' houses were sold.[10] If so, it was not enough to satisfy investors in the company. The modern look, in particular the flat roof, was unpopular among house buyers and mortgagors alike. Eventually the company abandoned its modernist ideals, influenced no doubt by its new partners, Sears Roebuck. Fisher left to take up a government post in 1940. Three years later, at the peak of wartime production, General Houses was producing 2,000 traditional-style houses per month from a chain of eleven factories in nine states.

The development of General Houses was paralleled by that of the only slightly more specifically named American Houses. The two companies were remarkably similar. American Houses was also founded in 1932 by an architect, Princeton-trained Robert W. McLaughlin Jr, and supported by wealthy industrialists including Owen D. Young. Its product, called the Motohome, looked very like General Houses's early modernist models and it too floundered for lack of demand despite a successful product relaunch in 1935 masterminded by Foster Gunnison, who was later to become a major manufacturer in his own right. In 1938, after Gunnison had left, the pragmatic McLaughlin realigned the company to produce traditional wooden houses, pre-cut and partially pre-assembled in its factory at South Kearney, New Jersey.

In quantitative terms, prefabrication's contribution to housing in the US in the 1930s was minor. But hopes that the industry might help solve the nation's economic problems prompted a number of important institutional and technical developments. Private research institutes like the John B. Pierce Foundation and the Albert Farwell Bemis Foundation became active (their publications are now among the main historical sources) and the government began to promote prefabrication through agencies such as the Farm Security Administration and the Tennessee Valley Authority. The most important technical development was the increasing availability of cheap manufactured boards like plasterboard, fibreboard and plywood. While go-ahead companies like General Houses and American Houses were experimenting with advanced steel structures and dimensionally co-ordinated systems, more conservative companies were using the new board products to make simple room-size

Motohome
Prototype, 1933.

timber-framed panels in the factory. Cheap, flexible and adaptable to any scale of production, panelization was a logical development from pre-cutting. More importantly the houses it produced were 'traditional' and therefore met less market resistance than the 'houses of the future'. Board manufacturers like Homasote promoted their own building systems designed for production by local timber yards using simple table jigs. The US Forest Products Laboratory meanwhile was researching new panel types, in particular stressed skin panels, which could be made thinner by taking into account the structural contribution of the covering boards as well as the supporting frame. There were also experiments in what were then called 'sandwich panels', triple-layer laminated panels that dispensed with the timber frame altogether – an early version of the modern Structural Insulated Panel (see Chapter 7).

Not all developments concerned the external envelope of the building. The Pierce Foundation developed a prefabricated 'mechanical core', basically a common wall between kitchen and bathroom to which all sanitary fittings and associated plumbing were attached, plus the heating and ventilating plant. American Houses adapted the idea for its Motohome, calling it the 'Moto-unit'. The kitchen part of the Moto-unit, with its base cupboards, wall cupboards, stainless-steel worktop, built-in cooker and refrigerator, extractor fan and overhead lighting, would be hard to improve even today.

Modular construction, then usually called 'sectional', was another technical development which, though not new, was given a push by government sponsorship. The huge civil engineering project to dam the tributaries of the Tennessee River was part of President Roosevelt's 'New Deal'. The dams were constructed in sequence, creating an awkwardly dynamic housing problem: how to accommodate the large workforce in reasonable comfort, quickly and for a limited period with the minimum of waste. Various methods were tried, including cheap disposable cabins and half-finished houses designed to be upgraded later for permanent use. But the solution for which the Tennessee Valley Authority became famous in the building world was the movable house, made in lorry-sized, box-like sections delivered to the site complete with all fittings and finishes and zipped together in twos, threes and fours to produce a range of types. When the dam was finished, the houses could be unzipped and carried to the next dam. It was a forerunner of the 'double-wide' mobile home and as such should perhaps form part of the separate history of that specialized form (see Chapter 3), but it was also influential on the mainstream development of prefabrication, in particular the British post-war temporary housing programme, of which more later.

'Prefabrication gets its chance' was the heading of an article in the February 1942 issue of *Architectural Forum*.[11] The National Housing Agency had allocated $153 million dollars for 'demountable' houses for workers in new armaments factories. 'Naturally', the article went on, '[the agency's] objective in assigning the bulk and most crucial of its post Pearl Harbor orders to the prefab industry is not to put house manufacture on the map as a potential rival of conventional house building technique, but it may have that effect.' And it did. There were about 100 prefabrication firms in production by the end of 1941, although many were inexperienced latecomers attracted by the federal funds. A government committee inspected 35 of them and declared itself reasonably certain that they were capable of delivering 27,450 houses in 90 days.[12] The total production of prefabricated houses in the whole of the previous decade had not exceeded 10,000 units. Prefabrication had indeed got its chance. In that same February issue, *Architectural Forum* listed 101 prefabricators, giving brief details of production capacities and structural types and including some photographs of houses. There is not an 'architectural' house among them. The majority are utterly traditional, single-storey, pitched-roofed, timber-framed 'Cape Cods'. The claimed production capacities are impressive, however: Perma-bilt homes, 35 houses per day; Home Building Corporation, 'fabricates a plywood panel system with a prefabricated moto-unit', 160 houses a month; Gunnison Housing Corporation, 8 houses a day; E. F. Hodgson Co., 'the oldest prefabricator in the US', 200 houses a month; and so on.[13]

National Homes Corporation of Lafayette, Indiana, was typical. Founded in 1940, it had learnt from the mistakes of the 1930s pioneers. Its policy was not to mass-produce houses for a nation-wide market, but to concentrate on towns within a 480-kilometre (300-mile) radius of its factory. Before the government contracts had come along, its directors had built a profitable business selling mainly to individual families through a network of small builder/dealers. Its houses were cheap but of high quality and conventional in everything but their mode of production. Over the next 15 years, National Homes was to grow into the largest prefabrication firm in the country.

More than 200,000 prefabricated houses were built during the war, just over 12 per cent of total house production.[14] It was not a revolution, but it was a respectable showing. And there was more government help on the way. Housing for war workers was now replaced by housing for returning GIs as the national priority. In 1946 Wilson Wyatt was appointed as the government's 'housing expediter' and the Veterans Emergency Housing Act was passed giving him the power to control prices, allocate building materials and make loans to manufacturers. These were the government grants that Konrad Wachsmann and Walter Gropius were relying on to rescue their grandiose Packaged House project (see Chapter 1). Wilson called on the industry to produce 850,000 prefabricated houses in less than two years. This turned out to be over-optimistic. Only 76,400 were actually produced. Before the programme was complete Wyatt's policies had proved unworkable and he had been forced to resign.[15] But not before he had presided over the genesis of one final, over-ambitious, visionary project: the Lustron Home.

Carl Gunnard Strandlund had made his fortune and reputation running a farm equipment business in the difficult Depression years. In 1946 he was the boss of the Chicago Vitreous Enamel Products company, looking for applications for a new patented product: vitreous enamelled steel panels. In view of the post-war steel shortage, there were no government grants available for petrol stations and hamburger restaurants, but houses were a different matter. Strandlund approached Wilson Wyatt with an ambitious proposal to mass-produce steel houses. All he needed, he said, was $52 million capital and within nine months he could be producing 100 affordable houses a day. Wyatt believed him, gave the project his support and managed to secure a redundant aircraft factory outside Columbus, Ohio, on Strandlund's behalf. It proved more difficult, however, to persuade the Reconstruction Finance Corporation to provide the necessary capital and Wilson's failure to do so may have been one of the reasons for his resignation shortly after. It became clear, however, that President Truman was sympathetic to the project and in June 1947 Strandlund was given a massive $15.5 million loan. Against the political and financial odds, the project was suddenly viable.

Architect Morris H. Beckman, who had no experience of prefabrication, had already worked up Strandlund's sketches into a detailed design. The basic form of the Lustron house was conventional: an almost square single-storey with a recessed porch and a shallow-pitched, gabled roof. It was the construction that was unusual. The window frames, made by another manufacturer, were of aluminium, but almost everything else was steel. External walls, internal linings, even roof coverings, were made from porcelain enamelled steel panels. Walls were framed in light, pressed steel with doubled vertical studs to prevent 'cold bridging', and ceilings, also of enamelled steel, incorporated radiant heating. It was a straightforward translation of traditional

A Lustron home surviving into the 21st century.

A Lustron home under construction in 1949.

domestic form into a modern industrial material; a naïve answer, perhaps, to the question 'what would a house look like if you made it like a motor car?'

Naïve he may have been, but to make houses like motor cars was what Strandlund intended to do and he set about tooling up his factory accordingly, with moving assembly lines and every kind of automatic metal processing machinery. A nation-wide network of dealers was set up and an advertising campaign launched. People flocked to see the show houses built in strategic cities and for a while it seemed that the dream of the factory-made house had finally come true. Of course, it wasn't to be. Lustron had overreached itself before it even started production. Everything was wrong. The dealers were expected to buy the houses from the factory before they had sold them to the customer, the estimated 150 man-hours on-site construction time was more like 350 man-hours, and the idea that the lorry that delivered the house would leave its trailer behind as an on-site store while its tractor went to pick up an empty from a neighbouring site was a logistical nightmare. The biggest problem, however, was the technical design of the house. Made from about 30,000 small parts, it was far too complicated. For example, if the internal panels could be full height, why did the external panels have to be 2 ft (600 mm) square, with all the extra flanges, fixings and rubber joint gaskets that that entailed? Waste like this was pushing the price of the house up beyond what the target market could afford. And then there was the out of proportion investment in factory machinery, which included a massive press making steel baths at several times the necessary rate. Nobody could be persuaded to buy the surplus baths because they were a non-standard size. The architect and prefabrication expert Carl Koch was called in to sort out the mess and he made a start on a rationalization of the design, but it was too late. Having invested heavily in Lustron at the start, the government had continued to support it with further loans, not wishing to admit its poor judgement, but the company was plunging into debt, its financial affairs were in disarray and it was time to pull the plug. In March 1950 the Reconstruction Finance Corporation forced the company into bankruptcy and the assembly line stopped for good.

So the Lustron Home, which was invented by an experienced businessman, failed just like the Packaged House and the Wichita House, which were invented by architects. If anything Lustron failed even more spectacularly, which might, when combined with its political significance – the suggestion of corruption that is whispered around Strandlund's dealings with government – be enough to give it historical priority. But there is another, more straightforward reason why the Lustron is more important than the Packaged or Wichita houses. Where Wachsmann's and Fuller's projects had virtually no outcome in actual houses built, Lustron did at least manage to build 2,500 houses. It was a disappointing performance in view of early promises, but not negligible. And the people that bought those houses seem to have been very satisfied with them. Indeed a browse through the many Lustron-related websites indicates that a good number are still satisfied with them and cherish them with pride. The Lustron houses have lasted well and are still popular. And putting the three houses side by side – a Duralumin dome sliced up inside like a cake (the Wichita House), a two-bedroom bungalow in plywood (the Packaged House) and another in steel (the Lustron Home) – it is hard see how the more famous, architectural pair can claim superiority even in design terms.[16]

The AIROH house, sometimes known as the Aluminium Bungalow, is a fourth prefabricated house from the immediate post-war period that demands to be included in this survey. But first we should catch up with earlier developments in Britain.[17] Immediately after the First World War the British government encouraged non-traditional house construction as part of its 'Homes Fit for Heroes' policy. Material and labour shortages were acute but it was considered essential that the house-building programme should deliver quick, visible results in order to prevent civil unrest. A Standardization and New Methods of Construction Committee was set up to consider alternatives and a number of systems were approved representing a wide variety of new materials and techniques, sometimes in strange combinations. One of the most successful was the Dorlonco system, promoted by the steel company Dorman Long. A framework of light, rolled steel angles was pre-cut and prepared in the factory for erection on site by unskilled workers. Sheets of expanded metal lath were then fixed to the outside of the frame by means of intermediate steel rods and the whole exterior was cement rendered. The internal lining was of clinker concrete blocks, plastered. The houses were two-storey and traditional-looking, with pitched roofs and Georgian-style sash windows. It is hard now to reconstruct the logic of this form of construction. Its steel frame seems structurally redundant given the blockwork lining, and the cement render seems doomed to fail, which it duly did in the years to come. Shrinkage cracks let in the water, which rusted the steel, which forced the render off in large flakes. But about 10,000 Dorlonco houses were built by local authorities all over the country in the early 1920s.

The Dorlonco seems almost rational in comparison with the Duo Slab system, developed by William Airey and Sons Ltd. Site-cast horizontal concrete slabs formed cavity walls between *in situ* concrete columns cast in wooden formwork. Once again the houses were completely traditional in form. More than 4,000 were built and they proved remarkably durable. To understand these curious systems we have to bear in mind the shortage of skilled labour and the absence of any machinery on site. Everything had to be capable of being manhandled and assembled by a trained labourer. The 'site-prefabrication' principle of the Duo Slab system was actually rather ingenious. Le Corbusier was adopting a similar approach at the time with his Monol and Citrohan houses (see Chapter 1), although without anything like the same success in production terms. Several steel-clad houses were also developed, among them the Weir, the Atholl and the Cowieson, which used timber frames faced with flat (not corrugated) steel plates. More than 1,500 Weir houses were built, despite resistance to them from building unions.

Britain's post-First World War prefabricated housing was the most advanced in the world and was watched with interest in Germany and the US. In Britain, however, it was seen only as a temporary solution and interest faded when in the mid-1920s, sooner than expected, skilled labour and traditional materials came back on stream. The government had never been fully committed to prefabrication, always insisting that normal construction would be resumed as soon as possible.

It was no different after the Second World War. Similar conditions prevailed and a big, visible housing programme was called for. It came in October 1944 when the government allocated £150 million for the provision of temporary houses. Why temporary? Brenda Vale, in her authoritative study of the programme, suggests three reasons: first, to persuade the public to accept small, two-bedroom houses built by unconventional means; second, to placate the building unions and reassure traditional building workers that their skills were being reserved for a permanent housing programme; and third, because the houses were going to be paid for by a central government that had no wish to trespass on the territory of local authority housing providers in the long term.[18] An experimental temporary bungalow, called the Portal, after Lord Portal, the Minister of Works, had already been built and exhibited to the public. It was single storey and vaguely American looking, with its shallow pitched roof and big windows. It was also fitted with a prefabricated kitchen/bathroom assembly very similar to the one developed by the Pierce Foundation in the US. Unfortunately the Portal was made of steel and plywood, both materials in short supply, so it was never produced in volume, but it served as the basic prototype for all of the other models. They were eleven in number but only four were produced in quantity: the steel-framed and asbestos cement-clad Arcon; the timber-framed Uni-Seco; the pre-cast concrete Tarran; and, most successful numerically and most interesting technically, the aluminium AIROH.

AIROH stands for Aircraft Industries Research Organization on Housing. Like the Packaged, Wichita and Lustron houses, the AIROH house was designed to make use of spare capacity in the aircraft industry. Made in five factories scattered around the country, it was that rare thing in the history of the prefabricated house: a truly mass-produced product. Moving assembly lines that had once made Spitfires now made AIROHs at the rate of one every twelve minutes, not as pre-cut frames or panels, but in complete sections, including floors, walls and roof. Each house was made up of four sections, just like the larger houses made by the Tennessee Valley Authority. (The influence was conscious and direct. A contemporary description by W. Greville Collins specifically thanks the US embassy for providing information on the TVA houses.)[19] Wall panels of aluminium sheet riveted to extruded aluminium frames were filled with aerated cement for insulation and lined internally with plasterboard. Roofs were also made from aluminium sheet, in two layers, resting on aluminium trusses. Only the floors were of conventional timber construction. The plan was adjusted so that the standard Ministry of Works

AIROH demonstration house, opening ceremony.

Site assembly of the AIROH house above.

kitchen/bathroom assembly, which included a cooker and a refrigerator, could be fitted into one section. All plumbing and wiring was installed in the factory. When the four sections arrived on the site by lorry, they were positioned on dwarf walls using a special collapsible gantry, and bolted together through ingenious self-positioning connector blocks.

By housing standards, this was advanced technology yet it looked ordinary, neither technological nor architectural. Everyone over 40 brought up in Britain knows what a 'prefab' looks like, but very few could distinguish between a relatively primitive Arcon and a high-tech AIROH. A few prefabs still survive, far exceeding their ten-year life expectancy. They are looked upon now with affection and nostalgia and at least five have found their way into museums. But they were always popular. That vaguely American look, the fact that they were detached and single-storey with generous gardens, above all the

The Shrublands prefab estate in Great Yarmouth, Norfolk.

high standard of equipment, including even a refrigerator; this made them, for some at least, the symbol of happy post-war family life. Prefabs were built all over the country, some on small pockets of land such as bomb sites and allotments, some in big estates designed for later conversion to permanent housing. They were expensive, especially the AIROHs, which by 1947 were costing £1,610 each. That was more than permanent housing and it didn't take into account the cost of manufacturing plant. In American free-market conditions the whole temporary housing programme would probably have failed. The total production figures are impressive nevertheless: 156,623 prefabs, of which 54,500 were AIROHs.[20]

As far as permanent housing was concerned the government's basic policy was the same as it had been after the First World War: to return to normal building practice as soon as possible and in the meantime explore the possibilities of prefabrication.[21] An Interdepartmental Committee on House Construction was set up to look into alternative systems, just as its First World War counterpart had done. A number of systems were approved, of which the most successful was the steel-framed house promoted by the British Iron and Steel Federation (BISF). Like the Dorlonco house, the BISF house was assembled from a mixture of prefabricated and site-built elements in a variety of

BISF houses at Northolt, Middlesex, 1945.

materials. The rolled steel structural frame was rational enough, but the internal lining was of site-built concrete blockwork and the outer walls were of brickwork up to first-floor level only. The upper storey was clad in profiled steel sheets. Yet another technology was introduced for the first-floor deck: 50 mm (2 in) of *in situ* concrete on expanded metal lath. Ceilings were of site-applied plaster, also on expanded metal lath. This description applies to the prototype built at the government's Northolt demonstration site and techniques may have been modified in later production models, but it remained a curious concoction, a 'traditional' house made from completely non-traditional elements, except the brickwork, which was non-load-bearing. Nevertheless, about 30,000 BISF houses were built between 1946 and 1951.

The Airey Duo Slab system also had its 1940s equivalent, called the New Airey Duo Slab, although the form of construction was actually quite different. The *in situ* columns were dispensed with and the pre-cast concrete slabs were made in the factory, not on site. Concrete posts were first set up, supporting steel floor joists and roof trusses in a two-storey 'goal post' arrangement. Horizontal pre-cast slabs were then attached to the outside of this structure in the manner of clapboarding or tile hanging. Internal linings were of either plasterboard on a timber frame with glass fibre insulation, or concrete blockwork. The concrete components were made in nine factories, including Airey's own factory in York. There was an urban version of the house with a flat roof and a far more popular rural version with a steeply pitched gable roof. Many

Airey houses at Chingford, Essex, 1946.

of these houses survive and, despite their unconventional construction, have mellowed into almost picturesque additions to small villages all over the country. Most were built by local contractors who could buy the components from the nearest factory at advantageous rates under a government scheme. About 26,000 Airey houses were built in the period up to 1955.

Brian Finnimore lists 27 building systems operating in Britain during this period.[22] Numerically, the most successful were the *in situ* concrete systems, such as Wimpey No Fines (so called because the lightweight concrete mix contained no sand) and Laing Easiform. Together they contributed more than 100,000 houses up to 1955 and continued to build in volume well into the 1970s. The industrial boom town of Coventry gave over practically its whole house-building programme to Wimpey, celebrating the opening of the six thousandth No Fines house in the city in 1958. These were not, of course, strictly speaking prefabricated houses, although the reusable, see-through metal formwork was factory made in standard sizes and the whole operation was rationalized in a quasi-industrial way. Whereas the BISF and Airey systems were based on a single house type, No Fines offered more freedom. Eleven different house types were used on the Willenhall estate in Coventry. Needless to say, most No Fines houses were completely traditional in appearance – the usual two-storey cottages with pitched roofs, even when planned as flats.

Can these cottage-style post-war houses be described as 'architecture'? Were there any architects involved in their production? Yes, there were. For example, Frederick Gibberd, later to become famous as the planner of Harlow New Town and the designer of Liverpool Roman Catholic Cathedral, was responsible for the 'architectural treatment' of the Type B BISF House. Many progressive architects, including F.R.S. Yorke, Hugh Casson and Grey Wornum, supported prefabrication in principle. But there was a feeling among them that in the long run the traditional cottage style would not do. D. Dex Harrison, an architect who compiled a comprehensive survey of prefabrication for the Ministry of Works in 1945, wrote this about post-First World War houses such as the Weir and the Dorlonco:

> No attempt had been made to evolve designs which suited, and took advantage of, the new structural concepts. So utterly bankrupt was the movement in this respect that the new constructions were laboriously worked to the same niggling plans which were in common use for brick houses at the time.

And further on:

> This grim picture of failure to achieve a happy aesthetic result in the new constructional medium is relieved by the work of a few brilliant architects such as Gropius in Germany, Neutra in America and Beaudouin and Lods in France.[23]

In the mid-1950s architects who would have agreed with Harrison were gaining influence in central and local government. At the same time, one particular form of prefabrication, the large pre-cast concrete panel, was proving to be the cheapest system of all. It was best used not for cottages but for medium and high-rise blocks of flats. Bigger buildings and higher densities meant that large items of equipment such as tower cranes could be used economically. Pre-cast concrete also meant faster production, which suited the government's political purposes. And it appealed to the architects, who could imagine themselves to be realizing Le Corbusier's Utopian urban visions of the 1920s and '30s. The story of British prefabrication from 1955 to 1968, when a gas explosion partially demolished an East London tower block called Ronan Point and effectively brought the episode to an end, has been told many times. It is part of the history of prefabricated housing rather than the history of the prefabricated house. Perhaps its importance has been overemphasized. Finnimore describes it as 'a short lived and comparatively limited phenomenon'.[24]

There was an 'overshoot' of production after the Ronan Point disaster and the peak year for pre-cast concrete was in fact 1970, when 25,556 dwellings were built.[25] Six years later the commonest form of prefabrication was timber frame. The usual explanation for the late development of timber frame in Britain is that, as an imported material, wood was always expensive. This is unconvincing given that in the traditional load-bearing brick house almost everything except the solid parts of the external walls is made of wood. A simple enclosure framed in 100 by 50 mm (4 by 2 in) studs would be a small addition to the large volume of wood already used in floors, roofs, ceilings, partitions and joinery. This British ignoring of timber frame is something of a mystery, but the fact is that, apart from a few imports from Scandinavia, timber frame was not much used in England and Wales until the mid-1970s.

The big advantage of timber over steel or concrete for prefabrication is that it does not require a large investment in factory plant. One of the most successful British timber-frame systems of the 1970s was Frameform, promoted by James Riley and Partners. The system consisted of little more than a set of standard construction details. Local authority clients could design their own house types and send them to Frameform to be detailed. In theory plans had to conform to a standard grid but really this was just a token gesture designed to appeal to system-minded architects (see Chapter 6). The manufacture of components was subcontracted to a string of small workshops and assembly on site was carried out by teams of approved erectors. The houses were traditional in form, although at this period vaguely modernist in detail. Those that were clad in a single skin of brickwork were indistinguishable from site-built houses. Clients now included speculative builders as well as local authorities. Timber frame was the only type of prefabrication to be adopted enthusiastically by private builders and at its peak in the late 1970s it accounted for about 15 per cent of production. Soon afterwards, however, it suffered its equivalent of Ronan Point. In May 1983 Granada Television broadcast a 'World in Action' documentary based on worrying reports of technical failures in timber-framed houses, mostly caused by bad workmanship and hidden condensation. It was big news and buyers of new houses immediately began to insist on proper load-bearing brick walls. Trad had triumphed again and prefabrication had suffered a set-back from which it only began to recover in the late 1990s.[26]

Meanwhile in the US, where timber frame was normal and houses were built almost entirely by private enterprise, the level of prefabrication had settled at about 10 per cent of total house production by the mid-1950s, although there were wide variations from one part of the country to another. In certain parts of the Midwest the proportion was more like 50 per cent. Companies like National Homes of Lafayette, Indiana, and Sholz Homes of Toledo, Ohio, sold both to individuals and developers. Technically their houses were unremarkable, basically panellized timber-frame structures in traditional styles. The

Typical US prefab house by National Homes.

differences lay in the scope of the package offered, whether it included built-in kitchen cabinets, for example, or a central heating system. Occasionally, big marketing campaigns were launched in both the consumer and technical press to promote certain brands, but the hoped-for revolution never took place. By the late 1960s prefabrication seemed to be in decline as the housing boom came to an end and conventional site building became more competitive.

But by then another type of prefabricated dwelling, half house, half vehicle, was racing past the slowing traffic to take the lead.

# 3. House of the century: the mobile home

Ward and Jeanne Belford, a retired couple in their youthful seventies, live in a house by an isolated lake in rural Wisconsin. Ward built the house himself. But every year in the late autumn, before the snowy winds come, they pack their car and drive 3,500 kilometres (1,900 miles) south to the Gulf coast of Florida, there to relax in the balmy air and reliable sunshine until Easter. Both worked in the telecommunications industry, Ward as an engineering manager and Jeanne as a director of human resources. In 1991 they rented a site in Southern Pines, a 379-home retirement community on the inland side of Highway 41, and ordered a house to be built on it. Southern Pines is a gated community for the over-55s. The gate is controlled by an answerphone device set at car-driver level (nobody would ever walk here) and supervised by a CCTV camera with its own channel on the community's cable service. Security systems are maintained by the private owners of the community, who are also responsible for lawn mowing and rubbish removal. There are strict rules forbidding yard ornaments, pick-up trucks and clothes-lines. Whether an American flag counted as a yard ornament became a topic for debate in the weeks after 9/11.

Gated communities are designed to keep people out while controlling the behaviour of the few who are let in, but they also have a more positive aim: to promote friendship and neighbourliness among the residents. Though Ward and Jeanne drive a big Chrysler Town and Country Van and keep a pontoon boat for Gulf-water fishing and cruising, they occasionally take advantage of Southern Pines's on-site recreational facilities. These include a large colonial-style clubhouse, which has a reading room like a country house library, a variety of games rooms, lounges and dining-rooms, and an enormous porch overlooking a lake. Outside there's a swimming pool, tennis courts, a putting green and a shuffleboard court.

Ward and Jeanne's house is single-storey, spreading wide and low on its patch of lawn as if it too were relaxing in the sunshine. This is no holiday

Manufactured homes at the Southern Pines community, Florida.

cottage, but a large and luxurious home with two bedrooms, two bathrooms, a lanai or sunroom fitted out as a television room, a washhouse, a carport, a study in which Jeanne can pursue her genealogy hobby on her computer, and a workshop in which Ward can make his model aeroplanes. Only a tutored eye would guess that it had been towed to the site in two prefabricated sections, each with its own steel chassis and wheels. It took just a couple of days to zip the two sections together, mount them on blockwork pier foundations and connect them up to local services. For this is a 'manufactured home'. The innocent-sounding phrase was coined in the 1970s as a euphemism for 'mobile home', which in turn was a euphemism for 'trailer', or what the British, failing to make any distinction between a permanent dwelling and a little metal box towed behind a family car, insist on calling a 'caravan'. Ward and Jeanne shopped around for their manufactured home among the dealers representing such well-known manufacturers as Fleetwood, Champion, Skyline and Palm Harbor, but eventually ordered one direct from Jacobsen Homes in Tampa. They looked at the standard range of about 50 floor plans, but in the end devised their own plan within the maximum 66 by 28 ft (20 by 8.5 metre) envelope of a two-section, or 'double-wide', configuration. Lanai and carport were site-assembled extras added to the main volume. The house cost $88,000 and Ward reckons that this was anything from $30,000 to $60,000 cheaper than a conventional site-built house of similar proportions.

An hour's drive away, at Palm Harbor Homes's factory on the edge of Plant City, a dozen potential customers just like Ward and Jeanne are collecting their popcorn before entering the little cinema. The marketing people at Palm Harbor know exactly what is uppermost in the mind of anyone contemplating buying a manufactured home. That's why the standard factory tour begins with a film about Hurricane Andrew. There is a myth that manufactured homes, which everyone knows are really trailers in disguise, have the magical power to attract tornadoes and hurricanes. There have been so many news pictures of manufactured homes bowled over or reduced to piles of matchsticks. Cameramen probably seek them out deliberately. On 24 August 1992, when the eye of Hurricane Andrew hit the town of Homestead about 48 kilometres (30 miles) south of Miami, the myth came true. Most of the 1,176 mobile and manufactured homes in the community known as Gateway were completely destroyed. The film boasts that of the ten Palm Harbor homes on the Gateway site, eight came through with only minor damage. But the broader message is that Gateway was unlucky, that site-built houses would have fared no better, and that in any case regulations have now been stiffened and specifications improved.

The factory tour that follows the film confirms that structurally a manufactured home is just as solid (or just as flimsy) as a conventional timber-framed house. The technology is essentially the same, apart from the steel chassis. Surprisingly, chassis are purpose-made for each house, not standardized. Different house plans have different load distributions, which are balanced by cambering or pre-stressing the steel members. The floor, which is made of ordinary 8 by 2 in (200 by 50 mm) joists laid across the steel chassis, is constructed first, complete with drainage and water supply pipework. Walls are made on a flat jig with door and window sub-frames in place and thick 'bats' of pink glass-fibre insulation pushed in between the studs. Unusually, a Palm Harbor house uses 6 by 2 in (150 by 50 mm) wall studs, not the 2 by 4 that is almost universal in all American timber-framed housing and has been for 150 years. Bigger studs means more hurricane resistance and thicker insulation, but more importantly it is a 'USP' (unique selling property), like the 'Dura Beauty' finishes options, the 'Energmiser' energy management system and the 'Gold Key' aftercare service. When the walls and roof have been hoisted into position, a gang of electricians moves in, rapidly fixing the power and lighting circuits from the outside of the building, something that would be almost impossible in a site-built house. External plywood sheeting and internal drywall linings are applied next. Then, while the maintenance-free, through-coloured strip vinyl siding and thin glass-fibre roof shingles are being fixed to the outside, on the inside the kitchen cabinets are being fitted and the floor and wall finishes applied. By the time the house is moved out into the yard prior to delivery, it contains the particular appliances ordered by the customer – cooker, refrigerator, washing machine, dishwasher – and it even has curtains at the windows.

Palm Harbor's Plant City factory.

Skyline manufactured home, ready for delivery.

'Double wides' awaiting final assembly on site.

The factory employs about 450 people but the production line is conceived on a modest scale. Units are dragged sideways from workstation to workstation on dollies attached to a simple chain pulley device, and there are travelling cranes overhead but, by Japanese standards for example, automation is minimal. You can still see men carrying lengths of timber on their shoulders. Any comparison with automobile production would be absurd. It takes about three days to make a complete house and this factory produces about five houses a day. Most are built to order. Possible variations on the standard types are almost infinite, but they all end up looking rather similar. The show houses ranged round the lake in front of the factory are distinguished from one another externally by superficial decorative features such as dummy dormers, fake-arched windows and stuck-on vinyl pilasters. The main aim seems to be to make them look as little like mobile homes as possible. But they all have the same shallow pitched roofs and the characteristic almost-flush eaves detail that is necessary to avoid exceeding the maximum width for road transport. Inside the plans vary considerably, although the restriction imposed by the standard 14 ft (4.27 metre) unit width is usually discernible.

The basic form and technology of the typical manufactured house seems primitive, yet this is a highly developed product, refined by customer demand and by decades of small improvements to the production process. Palm Harbor constantly surveys its potential customers and makes changes to its products every year. 'Design', however, hardly comes into it. There is a product development team and there are 'floor plan creators' but no one claims authorship of the design of a manufactured home. Asked if he ever calls upon the services of an architect, factory manager Dan Ziebarth scratches his chin and finally answers no, but he does consult an interior designer to find out what colours are currently fashionable.

The house-on-wheels has a long history stretching back well into the nineteenth century, to the Gypsy caravan in Europe and the covered wagon in America. But the continuous evolution of the mobile home proper began in the 1920s, when winter vacationing families from the north stocked their Model T Fords with tinned food and set off for the campgrounds of the south and west.[1] Some formed themselves into associations, like the Tin Can Tourists who met every year from 1919 at De Soto Park in Tampa, Florida. To qualify as a Tin Can Tourist you had to live in a tent, a converted car, a trailer or a temporary hut. Residents of Florida were not allowed to join. The essential features of the nascent mobile home industry were therefore already in place: the homes on wheels, the campground or park, the regulations, the exclusive identity. The technology of Tin Can Tourism was a do-it-yourself

Airstream trailer settling into a Florida park.

business. Car conversions ranged from simple awnings to elaborate enclosures with proper doors and windows. But the most convenient form was the trailer, because it could be unhitched, freeing the car for other duties. Early home-made trailers were built from wood and canvas, like the one made in the mid-1920s by Arthur Sherman, the president of a pharmaceutical firm in Detroit. It measured only 9 by 6 ft (2.75 by 1.83 metres), with a drop-down back forming a cooking space. So many people complimented Sherman on his trailer that in 1929 he rented a garage, employed two cabinetmakers and set up a production line. By 1936 his company, called Covered Wagon, was turning out 6,000 units a year and grossing $3 million. It was the biggest of about 400 manufacturers who together produced more than 80,000 'trailer coaches' a year.[2]

By now the trailer coach was beginning to adopt a fashionable, streamlined image. The more expensive models, like the Road Chief, the Silver Dome and the classic Airstream, were shiny aluminium teardrops reminiscent of aeroplanes or yachts. But the shining image was soon tarnished when, in the Depression years, what had been a symbol of fun and freedom became the only available home for the poor and the unemployed. For the first time, people started living in trailers permanently, colonizing patches of waste ground on the outskirts of cities. The campground became the trailer park, a phrase with very different connotations. Then in the early 1940s, as the nation geared up for war, the trailer home gained a kind of respectability, coming into its own as temporary housing for the military and for the migrant workers that swarmed around the armaments factories. Suddenly it was patriotic to live in a trailer. Private sales were forbidden by law and the government, urged on by the Trailer Coach Manufacturer's Association (TCMA), began buying trailers by the thousand. Approved models included the plywood and canvas 'Committee Trailer', so called because it was developed by three members of the TCMA's War Activities Committee, and the more elaborate Stout trailer, with fold-out extensions, designed by the engineer William Stout, who had been responsible for a number of classic industrial designs in the 1930s, including the Ford Trimotor aeroplane.

But the government always regarded trailers as a temporary expedient and when the National Housing Agency set minimum standards for war workers' housing in 1943, trailer homes were declared substandard. The TCMA now had to fight for the industry's right to exist, arguing for the resumption of private sales and struggling to re-establish a market. After the war, many of the surviving manufacturers wanted to forget the idea of trailers as permanent homes and re-establish the happy associations of their product with the freedom of the open road. The streamlined look reasserted itself, as if to insist that these were primarily vehicles, not houses. But working people and war veterans had got used to living in trailers, which were now firmly established as a low-cost housing option. Here was a market waiting to be developed. Designers struggled with the vehicle/house ambiguity, often combining the streamlined incongruously with the domestic. The main practical problem, however, was the 8 ft (2.4 metre) width restriction imposed by highway authorities all over the country. Fold-out and telescopic extensions were a possible solution, but they were expensive, awkward to use and not always weathertight. An eight-foot wide family house presented insuperable planning problems. There was no room for a corridor, so it was necessary to pass through one bedroom to get to the other – acceptable perhaps for a brief holiday, but not for permanent occupation. An extra two feet would make all the difference.

In 1954 Elmer Frey, the president of Marshfield Homes, did the obvious but almost unthinkable thing: he made a 10 ft (3 metre) wide trailer. In his book *Wheel Estate* (far more scholarly than its title suggests), Allan D. Wallis sees the introduction of the 'ten-wide' as a turning-point in the history of the mobile home.[3] It was the moment when the line between vehicle and house was crossed. You could get special permission to take a ten-wide on the road but you couldn't do it too often and you certainly couldn't go touring from state to state. The ten-wide was not a vehicle, it was a house. Its wheels and chassis were now just a way of moving it from the factory to the site. It might only ever make that one journey. At first the other manufacturers were reluctant to

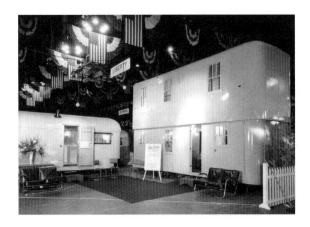

'Liberty' telescopic two-storey trailer, 1946.

Fold-down extendable trailer, 1954.

accept such a radical reformulation of their product. But then the implications began to sink in and the business opportunities began to gleam in the distance. Frey's ten-wide was still metal-clad and vehicle-like in appearance, but why? If it was a house, why shouldn't it look like a house? And if ten feet wide was acceptable, why not twelve? Or fourteen? The first twelve-wides were introduced in 1959, although most highway authorities held out against them until 1963. By 1969 the fourteen-wide had made its appearance.

John Steinbeck first became aware of the mobile home in 1960, as he toured the country in a converted pick-up truck with his dog, Charley. Invited to eat with a family of mobile home dwellers, he reconstructs the after-dinner conversation at some length. The father of the family has this to say on the question of roots and rootlessness:

> What roots are there in an apartment twelve floors up. What roots are in a housing development of hundreds and thousands of small dwellings almost exactly alike? My father came from Italy ... He grew up in Tuscany in a house where his family had lived maybe a thousand years. That's roots for you, no running water, no toilet, and they cooked with charcoal or vine clippings. They had just two rooms, a kitchen and a bedroom where everybody slept, grandpa, father and all the kids, no place to read, no place to be alone, and never had had. Was that better? I bet if you gave my old man the choice he'd cut his roots and live like this.

Later he shows Steinbeck some magazines for mobile home dwellers:

> . . . stories and poems and hints for successful mobile living ... Also there were full-page pictures of new models, each one grander and more shiny than the next. 'There's thousands of them,' said the father, 'and there's going to be millions.'[4]

And there were millions. But the mobile home couldn't go on getting wider. How could it be made more house-like while remaining mobile? The answer was the double-wide, each chassis bearing only a half a house, delivered to site with one side gaping open and its roof temporarily propped.

Only the chassis and wheels distinguished the double-wide from a prefabricated 'modular' house. This distinction was important, however. In 1976, with the full support of an industry now committed to becoming a housing provider, the US Department of Housing and Urban Development put into effect the Federal Manufactured Home Construction and Safety Standards, now known everywhere as the HUD Code. It effectively launched the modern concept of the manufactured home. Until then mobile homes had had to conform to local building regulations – an obvious contradiction in terms. But the HUD code applied only to structures built on permanent (not removable) chassis. This meant that in order to maintain the privilege of exemption from local building regulations, the mobile home was obliged to remain, in theory, mobile.

The coming of the ten-wide effectively split the trailer industry in two. One half stuck with the idea of real mobility, its trailers eventually becoming the luxury Recreational Vehicles of today, some designed to be towed by pick-up trucks, others self-propelled like the famous Winnebago. The other half of the industry settled down to its new role as an adjunct to the construction industry, developing its product accordingly. All concessions to mobility and lightness – the thin, metal-clad external walls, the cardboard partitions, the bouncy floors, the miniature ironmongery, the plastic sinks – were gradually designed out. Ordinary timber-frame construction technology was almost universally adopted, partly because it was cheap and simple, and partly because it was associated with 'proper houses'. An important part of this transformation was a change of name. 'Trailer' meant temporary housing for poor people. It had to go. In 1953 the Trailer Coach Manufacturers' Association became the Mobile Home Manufacturers' Association (MHMA). Twenty years later, 'mobile home' had picked up its share of negative associations and name inflation demanded another denomination. In 1975 the MHMA changed its name to the Manufactured Housing Institute, removing all reference to mobility and deliberately blurring its territorial border with the construction industry.

Much of the success of the mobile home as a housing form was due to the gregarious habits it had inherited from those early vacation campgrounds and from wartime concentrations around factories, shipyards and civil engineering projects. In the 1950s the MHMA recognized the potential of the mobile home park as a stimulus to demand and a guarantee of the health of the industry. Managing parks was a growing business and it was in the manufacturers' interests to give it every support. Would-be park owners were offered design consultancy services for a nominal fee and model plans were published to illustrate recommended lot sizes, road layouts, landscape treatments and service details. The MHMA called in landscape consultants from the Universities of Illinois and Michigan, but mostly the designs were developed on the basis of practical experience.

Two types of mobile home park began to emerge: those providing basic affordable housing, mainly for first-time buyers, and those providing additional services such as clubhouses, swimming pools and golf courses, often for prosperous retired people. The distinction still applies even though the mobile home has become the manufactured home and parks now look more and more like ordinary suburban housing developments. Housing-based parks typically accommodate economical single-wide starter homes, while service-based parks cater for luxury double-wides. In either case, the typical manufactured home dweller has to get used to life in what is basically a camp, with its own rules and restrictions representing a considerable curtailment of ordinary freedoms. This, for example, is what the rule book for Ward and Jean Belford's Southern Pines park has to say about guests:

Mobile home park planning model, Los Angeles, 1946.
Multi-storey mobile home park, St Paul, Minnesota, 1971.

All guests must be registered in the Guest Register in the Park Office, which states the owner's name, lot number, name of guest[s], arrival date and departure date ... Homeowners may have children as guests but for no longer than 15 days in any six month period except with the written permission of the park owner.

But this has to be seen against the background of the increasing tendency of well-off Americans, especially Florideans, to live in gated communities. The form may owe something to the trailer park in its origins, but it is no longer restricted to mobile and manufactured homes. In the last twenty years the landscape of inhabited Florida has become a patchwork of private residential zones, each branded and marketed by its developers to suit a particular stage or style of life. Categories include: Family, Active Adult, Senior Citizen, Golf and Country Club, not forgetting the special category, Open to All. So-called 'master-planned' communities take the gated community to its logical conclusion, including private shopping centres and schools so that residents never have to leave. In these 'subdivisions' lots are bought outright by residents, rather than rented as they usually are for manufactured homes, and the houses are ordinary, site-built structures. Even so, the similarities with the trailer park concept are striking.

About 40 per cent of mobile homes are sited in parks. Of the remainder, some simply take the place of site-built houses on individual suburban lots, but many perform a special function as a kind of lubrication in the machinery of housing provision. For example, mobile homes make excellent instant house-extensions. If newly weds can't afford to buy a place of their own, they can be accommodated in reasonable comfort in a mobile home parked in their parents' yard. And when mum and dad retire, they can swap places, turning the mobile home into a granny flat. In California mobile and modular granny flats are marketed under the acronym ECHO, which stands for Elder Cottage Housing Opportunity.

For many relatively poor Americans, owning a mobile home is an option much preferred to the alternative of an apartment in the inner city. Workers in the new industries of the south-eastern states (the Carolinas, Georgia, Tennessee and Virginia) have spontaneously created what geographers John Fraser Hart, Michelle J. Rhodes and John T. Morgan have called Spersopolis, 'the ideal populist city of the automobile age'.[5] Spersopolis takes the form of a network of very low density development extending for hundreds of miles over the rural landscape. Roads become necklaces of individual houses of every type, from luxury mansions to tumbledown shacks, but with a high proportion of mobile and manufactured homes. The manufactured home has even begun to exert an architectural influence in its own right. A new vernacular house type has emerged known as a 'half-house', which is essentially a self-built version of half of a double-wide.

The manufactured home is not necessarily an exclusively rural or suburban animal. In 1997 the Manufactured Housing Institute commissioned architects Susan Maxman and Partners to develop affordable house types

Two-storey manufactured home designed by Susan Maxman and Partners for urban sites.

for urban infill sites. Demonstration houses were built in Wilkinsburg, Pennsylvania, Washington, DC, and Louisville, Kentucky.[6] Many are two-storey, with steeply pitched, fold-out roofs and traditional site-built porch extensions, but they all have fixed chassis and conform to the HUD code. Two-storey manufactured homes are rare, but only slightly more awkward than single-storey to build and install. There are two methods. One single-storey module can be lifted onto another by crane on the site, with a slight modification to the chassis of the upper module. Alternatively, complete two-storey modules can be built in the factory, provided there are no low bridges on the road to the site. The Susan Maxman-designed houses are almost indistinguishable from their older, site-built neighbours. All traces of their vehicle parentage have been erased.

Given its quality, speed and cheapness, the manufactured home ought by now to have achieved blanket acceptance, as the balloon-frame house did in the nineteenth century. But this hasn't happened. The reason is that in housing, as in all architecture, objective measures are less important than history and public perception. The manufactured home may these days look like any other home, but everybody knows where it came from and it can't deny its roots. A common objection to mobile home parks used to be that their residents did not pay property taxes and were therefore parasites on the community. But this often concealed ordinary class and racial prejudice. Mobile home dwellers were usually poor and sometimes did not conform to suburban social conventions. Property prices were affected. The horrible phrase 'trailer trash' gained currency. Such prejudices persist to this day and are compounded by ignorance of the technology of the modern manufactured house. Its construction is thought to be inferior, although it is in fact essentially the same as that of any other timber-framed house.

It sometimes seems that the mobile/manufactured home was ever destined to be either despised or ignored by housing professionals. We have seen how the government turned against trailers in 1943, despite their evident usefulness. In 1969, in the wake of widespread urban riots, the Department of Housing and Urban Development launched Operation Breakthrough, designed to stimulate the development of industrialized building and thereby boost the production of cheap homes for the urban poor. Federal funds were allocated and demonstration projects were set up to test various new technologies. By the time Richard Nixon pulled the plug on the programme in 1973, $72 million of federal money had been spent to produce 25,000 dwellings. In the same period, the mobile home industry had quietly produced ten times that number with no federal help whatsoever. The answer to the affordable housing problem was right there under the noses of the politicians and civil servants, but it didn't count because it wasn't considered proper housing. In 1981 Ronald Reagan set up the Affordable Housing Demonstration Program to prove the positive effects of deregulation in the construction industry. Various projects were published, indicating average cost savings of about 16 per cent. On closer examination, however, it became clear that the savings were the result not of deregulation, but of the simple fact that the houses were smaller; pro rata, they were actually more expensive than their regulated counterparts. The manufactured housing industry meanwhile was routinely achieving savings of 30 per cent and more over conventional houses without fiddling the figures.

The manufactured home industry is itself somewhat ambivalent about the status of its products. On the one hand it wants them to be treated like ordinary houses, especially as far as zoning is concerned, but on the other it wants to maintain their distinctive reputation in the market for speed and affordability. This dilemma is summed up in the HUD code's insistence on a non-removable steel chassis, the distinguishing feature that is both the main strength of the manufactured home and the precise limit of that strength. Many manufactured home producers, including Palm Harbor, also make modular houses, with removable chassis, that are delivered to their sites on flatbed trucks. These houses evade the zoning restrictions that apply to true manufactured homes, but fall outside the provisions of the HUD code and are therefore subject to local building regulations. Swings and roundabouts.

At Palm Harbor, modular houses remain a sideline and do not challenge the dominance of the traditional product. This is because the manufactured house is more than just a product: it is a complex commercial, industrial and cultural system. The individual houses may seem illogical in their design and easy to improve, but they are only the fruit of the tree. To understand them, you have to look at the whole organism with its interdependent networks of suppliers, manufacturers, transport companies, dealerships and park owners, and at the commercial and regulatory environment that nourishes it. You have to notice the way that manufacturers benefit from the extended credit offered by suppliers of materials and components while taking cash-on-delivery from the house dealers; the way that the size of a manufacturing plant is governed not by the demands of mass production or the economies of scale but by the population of a catchment area limited by the distance a house can reasonably be towed in one day (anything up to 800 kilometres); the way that the specialized transport sector of the industry has evolved techniques to avoid 'empty back hauls'; the way that dealers generate a critical mass of potential customers by clustering their show-sites together in roadside 'trailer rows'; and the way that park owners are able to take advantage of the flexible, provisional nature of their investment, easy to finance and easy to convert to conventional development should the occasion arise.

Project Mobile Home Industry, the only large-scale academic study of the industry, was set up at Massachusetts Institute of Technology (MIT) in 1969 but did not publish its findings until 1980 in a book entitled *Building Tomorrow* by Arthur D. Bernhardt. Nobody could accuse Bernhardt of ignoring or despising the mobile home industry. He was its most enthusiastic fan. According to him it was 'the most efficient shelter industry in the world' and 'by far the most successful paradigm of the industrialization of building in all countries with market economies'.[7] The main reason for its success, he said, was precisely that it was not part of the construction industry; its base was and always had been the factory, not the building site. Basic business practices that the construction industry is still, to this day, struggling to understand – how to coordinate a supply chain or stimulate demand for a product – came as second nature to an industry that had begun in vehicle manufacturing. Bernhardt particularly admired the way that in the 1950s and '60s the industry had manipulated its commercial and regulatory environment, encouraging the development of mobile home parks and lobbying for the adoption of the HUD code. He admired its manufacturing methods too, especially the use of cheap, semi-skilled labour working together in small teams, a method that he rightly predicted would be 'the assembly line of the future'.[8]

But Bernhardt was not content just to admire and praise the object of his study; he wanted to make it even better and to apply its lessons to construction in general. He didn't see, for example, why the mobile home industry should be wedded to a relatively crude timber-frame technology. It ought, he thought, to consider new structural forms like post-and-beam or stressed skin, and new materials like light steel or even concrete. And why should the product range be limited to individual detached houses? Why shouldn't mobile home factories produce components for high-density cluster developments or urban infill projects, working in collaboration with traditional builders?

It was not a very convincing argument. On Bernhardt's own analysis, the industry was efficient because over the years it had developed its technologies and networks to a high level of refinement and compatibility. The last thing it needed was for someone to come along and change its products, its market and its method of distribution. It didn't need fixing. Bernhardt was unconsciously subscribing to the general social prejudice against the mobile home. Being the most efficient shelter industry in the world was not enough. It didn't count because the shelters in question were not real houses. What disqualified them from the status of real houses was not their size or quality but where they had come from and how they had got where they were. The subtitle of the book, *Housing Lessons from Mobile Homes*, reveals Bernhardt's position and that of respectable professional and academic commentators in general. The only reason to study the mobile home industry was to learn lessons from it and apply them elsewhere, in the real housing industry.

Architects, even those interested in mass-produced housing, have mostly ignored the trailer and the mobile home, too distracted by the shining example of the automobile to notice what was being towed behind it. And when they have noticed it they have tended, like Bernhardt, to want to change it, to turn it into architecture and make it respectable. In 1970 the architects of the Frank Lloyd Wright Foundation designed a Prairie-style mobile home. They simply took an ordinary ten-wide, added triangular bay windows at each end (living room and bedroom), a deep, three-layer, overhanging fascia, a couple of triangular planters, a terrace with angled steps, and a pergola. It was no more than a styling exercise, but at least it didn't interfere with the basic form. It could take its place in the pattern book along with all the other styles. Nobody seems to have wanted it, and it never went into production. Usually the mobile home's encounters with architects have far more radical outcomes, at least in theory. Archigram's 1967 proposal for a multistorey mobile-home park is typical of the tendency of architects to want to rethink the whole system. The drawing shows a suitably stylish selection of recreational vehicles, including

British Modernist mobile home of the 1970s.

Modular housing at New Haven, Connecticut, by Paul Rudolph.

several classic Airstreams, parked in what now looks like an ordinary multi-storey car park. It was supposed to be fun.[9]

Plugging living pods into multistorey megastructures has been a stock response of architects inspired by the possibilities of the mobile home. In the late 1960s Paul Rudolph, best known as the architect of the School of Art and Architecture at Yale University, began talking about the mobile home as 'the twentieth century brick'. Inspired more by its expressive than its functional potential, he designed a number of module/megastructure projects, the biggest of which was the so-called Graphic Arts Centre in Lower Manhattan, a massive mixed-use development including 4,050 'dwelling capsules' clustered in pin-wheel configurations around service cores rising to 50 storeys or more. The capsules were each 12 ft (3.6 metres) wide, for easy road transport, but folded out like the wartime Stout trailers to a width of 28 ft (8.5 metres). They were suspended by fire-protected steel cables from deep beams cantilevered out from the concrete cores. The scheme is mentioned with approval in Bernhardt's book, but it was never built. Rudolph did, however, build a low-rise version of it in New Haven, Connecticut, for Prince Hall Masons, an African American organization. The modules, similar to mobile homes but with curved plywood roofs, were arranged in two-storey pinwheels, the upper floor offset from the lower so as to create covered porches. Needless to say it was rather expensive, showing no saving on conventional construction.

'The mobile home by any other name', said Rudolph, 'could be a useful solution to the low-cost housing problem.'[10] Could be? Didn't he know that it already was? And note that distancing 'by any other name'. The patronizing attitude is summed up in this extract from an *Architectural Record* article about the Graphic Arts Centre:

> Rudolph believes that given the opportunity to properly design, upgrade and test its product ... the mobile home industry could become the leader in lightweight steel box frame technology, meeting this nation's and world's great need for handsome, well engineered, low-cost dwelling units.[11]

This is the advice that the author of a handful of modular housing projects, all but one of them unbuilt, offers to an industry that was at that time building more than half a million affordable homes a year.

The early 1970s was the heyday of the mobile home, but the decline that many predicted (including Alan D. Wallis) has not taken place. In 2000 manufactured homes accounted for 30 per cent of all new single family houses sold in the US, and in areas like Florida, and the south-east generally, the proportion is much higher. This is not surprising. If anything the figure is surprisingly small. In 1998 the cost per square foot of the average manufactured home was $31.89 – half that of a comparable site-built home.[12] The industry has not taken Arthur D. Bernhardt's advice and diversified into a wide range of new materials and structural forms. Instead it has cleverly adapted its cheap, simple product to suit a range of different markets, from luxury retirement homes to cheap single-wide starter homes and granny flats. Thousands of identical single-wides have been laid out in straight rows on open land to house the immigrant workforces of the hog farms and meat-packing factories of Kansas and Oklahoma. A typical 70 by 14 ft (21 by 4.27 metre) house in one of these brutally monotonous 'parks' has three bedrooms and two bathrooms and costs only $18,000. No other housing form comes close to the manufactured home for sheer volume, speed and value for money. At the same time, the industry is conducting experiments in sensitive urban infill and successfully customizing its product to appeal to the choosiest market sector in the world: well-off retired Americans like Ward and Jeanne Belford.

# 4. The question of authorship

Prefabrication, standardization, customization, mass marketing – the application of concepts such as these to building raises questions at a philosophical as well as a practical level. These questions can be profoundly unsettling for architects. They have the power to destabilize the very meaning of the word 'architecture'. And the most potent of them is the question of authorship.

In 1968 Roland Barthes wrote a now famous essay called 'The Death of the Author'. In it he puts forward the seemingly outlandish idea that novels, plays and poems are created not by authors but by readers. Of course he does not mean that novels write themselves. Someone has to pick up the pen and make the marks on the paper. But he calls this person a 'scriptor', a mere transmitter of meaning, not a creator of it. The scriptor is like the shaman in a tribal society, passing on or 'mediating' the traditional stories but taking no personal responsibility for them. The meanings of the stories are created, and constantly re-created, not by a single individual but by a whole society. Unlike the scriptor, the author is a named individual whose writing is assumed to be inseparable from his or her personality. The work of literature is interpreted and 'explained' by reference to its author's life history. *Paradise Lost* is read in the knowledge of Milton's blindness, *Pride and Prejudice* in the knowledge that Jane Austen never married. The author is seen as the originator or 'begetter' of the text, like a parent or an ancestor – or a god. The author's voice is the voice of 'authority'. But according to Barthes, this linking of the text to the voice of the individual author is false. 'Writing', he says, 'is the destruction of every voice, every origin.' It is not the author, but language itself that speaks. As soon as the author begins to write, he or she engages with the shared world of meaning and submits to the superior authority of the reader: 'The birth of the reader must be at the cost of the death of the author.'[1]

Barthes's ideas about authorship can of course be applied to other art forms such as painting and music. Can they be applied to architecture? Certainly they can. In fact the idea of the death of the author seems to apply more simply and directly to architecture than to any other art form. While it takes a degree of mental contortion to begin to think about literature, art or music without poets, painters or composers, the idea of architecture without architects is much easier to accept. Architecture is in practice a collaborative enterprise so the idea of the single author of a building seems doubtful from the start. The architect's first duty is to meet the needs of the client, who must surely therefore share in the building's authorship. The production of the detailed design, unless it is for a very simple building, is usually a team effort. There may be several architects involved, and engineers, surveyors and other consultants, not to mention town planners and building control officers, will all exert an influence. Most modern buildings, not just those described as 'prefabricated', are assembled from standard or semi-standard components. Sometimes the architect specifies proprietary systems for complete elements like structural frames, flat roofs and curtain walls. These components and systems have been designed by someone other than the architect. Should that person not also share in the authorship of the building? Building materials like bricks, tiles and sawn timber are also standardized, though by tradition rather than by conscious design. In what sense can an architect really be said to have 'designed' a brick wall? Finally, architects rarely construct their own buildings, and the process of building almost always involves negotiation and compromise resulting in modifications of the design.

The idea that a building should be credited to a single author seems on the face of it to be untenable, yet we continue to pay lip service to it. It is true that when detailed articles are written about buildings in professional journals there is often a separate panel in which all the consultants and contractors are listed (though in the case of the contractors, this is mainly to attract advertising). It is also true that even educated, well-informed members of the public find it hard to name more than two or three contemporary architects, so we are hardly in the realm of the film star. Nevertheless architecture seems to need the concept of authorship. Authorship is one of the things that distinguishes architecture from mere building. If the designer of a building cannot be identified, then that building's status as architecture is somehow called into question.

Authorship in architecture can create some weird distortions, both professionally and historically. For example, architects with a reputation for daring originality can sometimes develop strange notions about the extent of their authorship. Zaha Hadid, a brilliantly inventive architect but not known for her skill as an engineer, once designed a building (the Vitra Fire Station at Weil am Rhein, Germany) with an enormously elongated concrete canopy. In lectures about her work she would show slides of the canopy under construction, and of the absurdly dense lattice of steel reinforcing bars hidden within it, scornfully laying the blame for this heavy-handed structure at the door of the consultant structural engineers. She thus claimed authorship of the form of the canopy, but denied authorship of the means to make it stand up. In effect she was claiming an impossibly pure form of authorship that refused even to take account of one of the primary conditions of the building's existence, namely gravity.

The question of authorship can become very confused when buildings are designed by large architectural practices. Buildings are often attributed to the boss of the practice when in fact they were designed by relatively junior partners or employees. The boss may produce the first outline sketches and then pass them down to the drawing office in the traditional way, but it is not at all uncommon for the named author of the design to have played no part in it at all. Newspapers are usually unaware of this fact and professional journals, one of the most important sources of architectural history, tend to either ignore it or resort to sophistry in order to preserve the precious concept of authorship. It will be argued, for example, that the building was designed in accordance with certain principles or traditions unique to the practice and should therefore still be attributed to the named principal. Sometimes an anonymous designer becomes too prolific, the pressure becomes too great and it is necessary to bring them out of the back room and accord them the status of named author. This is how, for example, Gordon Bunshaft emerged from Skidmore, Owings and Merrill in the 1950s, Peter Foggo from Arup Associates in the 1970s, and Ken Shuttleworth from Norman Foster and Partners in the 1990s.

But it is in architectural history that the distortions caused by the concept of authorship do the most damage. Architectural history, like the history of any art form, is extremely selective. There are millions of buildings in the world but only a tiny proportion is recorded in the history books. Once a building has made it into one book, the odds against it appearing in another are drastically shortened. Gradually it becomes part of the artistic canon, the pool of familiar examples that historians and theorists draw on to illustrate their ideas. Admission to the canon depends to some extent on the quality or originality of the building, but if it was designed by a famous architect then its chances of admission are greatly improved. In a few extreme cases this circular process by which canon creates fame and fame creates canon reaches a lift-off velocity and a genius is born. Once an author attains the status of genius, then anything produced by that author automatically becomes canonical, regardless of its quality or originality. An example from the oeuvre of Le Corbusier might illustrate this point.

One of the most admired of Le Corbusier's late works is the Dominican monastery of Ste Marie de La Tourette, near Lyons, completed in 1961. The client for La Tourette, Father Alain Couturier, was a great admirer of the architecture of the medieval Cistercian abbey of Le Thoronet, near Toulon. What impressed Couturier most about Le Thoronet was its cloister, a calm, static, sheltered space of contemplation, and he drew attention to this precedent in his brief to Le Corbusier. Le Corbusier visited Le Thoronet, but does not seem to have been much impressed by the cloister because, when he began designing La Tourette, he chose to position the building on a steeply sloping part of the site that made

The monastery of La Tourette by Le Corbusier.

The Cistercian abbey of Le Thoronet.

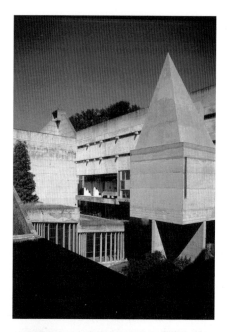

La Tourette by Le Corbusier, courtyard and pyramid-roofed oratory.

La Tourette, 'Mitrailleuses' in the roof of the sacristy.

the construction of a conventional cloister prohibitively expensive. His idea was to put the cloister (in the narrow sense of a continuous walkway around a court-yard) on the roof. This was part of an even bolder idea, which was essentially to turn the conventional monastery upside down. The level roof line became an inverted ground line, with two storeys of monks cells below and the various communal spaces – church, chapels, refectory and so on – 'hanging' over the undisturbed hillside. A sketch of this basic idea was passed to one of the senior assistants in Le Corbusier's office, a Greek political refugee called Iannis Xenakis, who began the long struggle to make the idea work. Circulation was a big prob-lem and Xenakis proposed several possible solutions, including a spiral ramp in the courtyard. At some point in the development process it became clear that the rooftop cloister idea was not what the client had in mind and would not be acceptable. In the end the circulation problem was solved by the introduction of a cross-shaped corridor into the courtyard, steeply ramped to accommodate changes of level.[2] This device was then designated 'the cloister', although it would be hard to imagine anything less like a cloister (except perhaps a rooftop walkway). Xenakis was no mere technician; he was an artist. His *métier*, howev-er, was not architecture but music: he was a pupil of Olivier Messiaen and, after he left Le Corbusier's office on the completion of La Tourette, he became an internationally renowned composer. Xenakis's musical leanings are apparent in certain prominent features of La Tourette, such as the so-called *ondulatoires* – storey-height window mullions spaced not regularly (as Le Corbusier had sug-gested) but according to a sequence of musical intervals. And consider this description of the genesis of two of the building's most photographed features:

> I drew a design with the chapel in the form of a grand piano, the organisa-tion of the light and so on as it is now ... Those were the cannons of light. Then I designed the orientation of the south wall of the sacristy, pentago-nal windows called 'mitrailleuses' – machine guns. Through them the sun falls directly inside only twice a year at equinox. I wanted to fix that, to tie it to astronomy.[3]

This is Xenakis speaking, not Le Corbusier. It has been suggested that the can-nons and machine guns are an echo of Xenakis's wartime experiences in Greece, when he was wounded by shrapnel.

The authorship of La Tourette is thus called into question. We begin to wonder which parts were by Le Corbusier and which by Xenakis, and we begin to see the building in a different light. Those *ondulatoires* suddenly look rather abstract and over-literal in their attempt to translate music into architecture. And the light cannons: aren't they a little too gestural, too much like bad sculpture? How many other features of the building are by Xenakis? The strange, finger-like concrete supports beneath the building have always looked out of place. What about the awkward way that the building sits on the site, perversely refusing that direct access from interior to exterior at ground level that is such an essential feature of any real cloister? The stark concrete interior of the church is undoubtedly impressive, even terrifying, as the door slams shut behind you and echoes for half a minute. But it is also rather like the inside of a water tank. (Xenakis proposed a lining of pyramid-shaped panels that would have improved the acoustic and completely changed the appearance of the interior but it was cut for lack of funds.) Which interpretation should we choose? It depends whether you look upon this building as a late masterpiece by an acknowledged genius, or as a deeply flawed early work by an artist who had chosen the wrong profession. The latter seems more plausible.

Yet this is a building that has been praised to the skies by critics and historians. Here, for example, is Robert Furneaux Jordan's verdict of 1972:

> And yet – and this is the whole key to La Tourette – in spite of plain forms, rough and unfinished surfaces, the sparing use of colour, the absence of all ornament and all images except the body of Christ on the Altar cross – Le Corbusier endowed La Tourette with a richness which seems to be not of this world. It is mysterious and intangible.[4]

The 'rough and unfinished surfaces' are usually interpreted as having a symbolic significance – like the rough cloth of a monk's habit – but in fact the concrete was left raw because there was not enough money to pay for the intended smooth cement render. And here is Colin Rowe writing about the author of La Tourette in the *Architectural Review* article of 1961 that set the tone of critical reaction to the building in Britain:

> Like the epoch, the man has his style – the sum total of the emotional dispositions, the mental bias and the characteristic acts which, taken together, comprise his existence.[5]

The man in question is of course Le Corbusier, not Iannis Xenakis.

The point here is not that the building has been misattributed (although it certainly has – Le Corbusier himself called it 'Le Couvent de Xenakis') but that critical interpretation of it has been skewed by the assumption that it was designed by the most important modernist architect of the twentieth century. Critics have seen what they wanted to see and turned a messy montage into a masterpiece.

So from where did the idea of authorship come? According to Barthes, authorship in literature was born in the Renaissance, and this theory will do equally well for architecture. It is not necessary to undertake years of research in primary sources to confirm that architectural authorship was born in the Renaissance, since it is history as written that influences current perceptions, not history as it really happened. And it is perfectly clear from any one of a dozen popular chronological surveys of Western architecture that when their writers reach the fifteenth century they begin to organize their material biographically rather than stylistically. Typically a chapter on late Gothic styles (Rayonnant in France, Perpendicular in England, Polychromatic in Italy) is followed by a chapter on fifteenth-century Florence. After a couple of introductory paragraphs, there is a trumpet fanfare and in steps Filippo Brunelleschi who, although he may not be the first named architect in the book, is nevertheless the first architectural author in the Barthesian sense. We learn about his quarrels with Ghiberti over the building of the dome of Florence Cathedral, his trip to Rome to study the methods of the Ancients, his demonstration of the principles of perspective that were so crucial to the artistic development of painters like his friend Massaccio. The narrative then continues on the well-worn path from author to author: Alberti, Bramante, Raphael, Michelangelo, Giulio Romano, Palladio, Bernini, Borromini and so on through the remaining chapters of the book until we arrive at the twentieth-century masters, Frank Lloyd Wright, Walter Gropius, Mies van der Rohe and Le Corbusier.

It isn't that the names of pre-Renaissance architects are unknown. We know, for example, that William of Sens designed the choir of Canterbury Cathedral and that, two hundred years later, Henry Yevele and Stephen Lote designed the nave. But that word 'designed' seems out of place. Historians tend to say 'built' in a medieval context because men like William, Henry and Stephen are considered to have been masons rather than architects in the modern sense. They were well educated, they spoke Latin and could probably hold their own in intellectual conversations with their learned clients, but their power base was the mason's yard and their worth lay in their knowledge of practical construction. Design (*disegno*) was a later, Renaissance idea, an abstraction, a separation of the form of a building from its substance and its construction. The rise of design is closely connected with the revival of classical forms. How could the 'new' antique style have been introduced by masons locked into a centuries-old medieval tradition of building in stone? A new kind of mason was required: a designer and an architect. Architecture began to drift away from construction and became identified with the new concept of design.

Renaissance architects were trained in a variety of professions. Brunelleschi was a goldsmith; Alberti was a scholar and dilettante, the original 'Renaissance man'; Antonio da Sangallo, exceptionally, was a carpenter. But most were artists – painters and sculptors like Raphael and Michelangelo. And they were heroes and geniuses in their own time, not just in the retrospective view of history. We know so much about them, not just as artists but as people, because they were celebrated by their contemporaries. Antonio Manetti wrote his biography of Brunelleschi in the 1480s and Giorgio Vasari, himself a painter and an architect, published his *Lives of the Most Excellent Painters, Sculptors and Architects* in 1550, when Michelangelo was still alive. It is dangerous to generalize about a subject as complex as the rise of the artist in the Renaissance, but there is no doubt that the foundations of the modern concept of architecture as an art form were laid then, and cemented in by later historians.

The divorce of architecture from construction was a necessary precondition for the rise of architectural authorship. But it was never a complete separation, never wholly a question of designers drawing their dreams and builders making them stand up. The perfect marriage of construction and architecture represented by medieval Gothic in its purest form was never achieved again, but there were many attempts to effect a reconciliation, most obviously in the nineteenth-century Gothic Revival. A.W.N. Pugin, the chief theorist of the movement, famously stated that 'there should be no features about a building which are not necessary for convenience, construction or propriety' and that 'all ornament should consist of the essential construction of the building'. This seems clear enough. Architecture should take its inspiration from construction: should be, in fact, no more than a faithful expression of it, as it had been in the Middle Ages. But there is a well-known logical flaw in this prescription, one that applies to all revivals. The medieval architect/constructors were continuing a live, unbroken tradition. A true re-creation of their situation would therefore not have resulted in any kind of *revival.* The Gothic Revival was an architectural, not a constructional idea. It was the nonnegotiable premise of the relationship between architecture and construction. The marriage was a sham. Architecture always wrote the rules.

It seems a big leap from the Gothic Revival to 1980s British High Tech, but there are similarities. Honesty of expression and truth to materials, for example, were articles of faith for High Tech architects. No faking was allowed: every part of the building had to do what it appeared to do and be made of the material it appeared to be made of. Pugin's prescriptions were perfectly acceptable to the High Tech architect. The ideological, and even the formal, similarities between High Tech and Gothic – Gothic, that is, filtered through nineteenth-century rationalism – have often been remarked upon. The big difference is that, whereas the Gothic Revival was an attempt to escape from the horrors of the industrial world into an idealized past, High Tech enthusiastically embraced industry. Factory production was an important theme, both as a practical expedient and as a source of imagery: take, for example, Norman Foster's Hong Kong & Shanghai Bank, Hong Kong, one of the two great culminating masterpieces of the High Tech style completed in 1987, the other being the Lloyd's Building in London by Richard Rogers.

The first thing anyone notices about the Hong Kong & Shanghai Bank is its curious 'coat hanger' structural frame, a kind of multilevel suspension bridge, boldly expressed on the outside of the building. If one of the quasi-Gothic rules of High Tech is that every feature of a building should have a functional justification, then what is the functional justification for such an elaborate tension structure? A conventional compression structure with ordinary columns and beams would certainly have been cheaper and simpler. The answer is that the structure, in conformity with the 'no-faking' rule, is exactly what it appears to be: a suspension bridge, creating a long, clear span over an existing banking hall carefully preserved from the old 1930s building. Except

Hong Kong & Shanghai
Bank by Norman Foster.

that the banking hall doesn't actually exist. The idea of preserving it was abandoned during the development of the design. The coat hanger structure is therefore an ingenious solution to a non-existent problem. When we have swallowed this, the next question is: why put the structure on the outside of the building when practical considerations (protection from the weather, ease of maintenance, simplification of the curtain wall details, cheaper fireproofing, elimination of differential deflection) would seem to demand that it should be on the inside? There is really only one reason why it should be on the outside: because it looks good. The point is that, although High Tech may look like engineering, its priorities are really quite different. When it comes to a showdown between architecture and practical construction, architecture usually wins. The visibility of the structure of the Hong Kong & Shanghai Bank is what makes it High Tech; it is what makes it 'architecture'; what makes it a Norman Foster building.

But perhaps the most interesting aspect of the Hong Kong & Shanghai Bank from the point of view of authorship is the concept known in the Foster office, rather blandly, as 'Design Development'. This means the design of factory-made building components by architects working in close consultation with manufacturers. It sounds unremarkable, but it is actually rather rare. Architects do not usually have much say in the detailed design of factory-made components. They merely make selections from catalogues, perhaps occasionally persuading the manufacturers to make minor modifications – a non-standard colour here, a slightly altered profile there. Design Development, however, is a much more thoroughgoing process, and one that is only really feasible on a big project with a big budget, like the Hong Kong & Shanghai Bank. All the major component systems of the building – curtain walling, structure cladding, service modules, ceilings, floors, partitions, and some of the minor ones like light fittings, handrails and toilet roll holders – were designed from scratch by Foster architects in collaboration with factory-based specialists. Mock-ups and prototypes were made and tested as if each system were a completely new product line.

Design development was heralded as a new partnership between architecture and industry. In truth it was a radical extension of architectural authorship into the factory. Versions of most of those component systems were already available in economical, semi-standardized forms designed by technicians who understood their materials, their machinery and their market. But they were not good enough. They had to be redesigned and made into architecture under the supervision of a Foster representative. They had to be assigned an architectural author. What resulted was one of the great buildings of the twentieth century, but it contributed little to the development of the

Specially designed floor components in the Hong Kong & Shanghai Bank.

construction industry because, quite simply, it was too expensive. It was a one-off; a monument to authorship; a dead end.

Architects seem to need authorship. It is what motivates them. They feel that they own their designs in a deeper sense than merely holding the copyright. Sometimes they assert their ownership even when it is against the interests of their client. Persuading clients to spend more than they wanted to on a design they don't really like is a skill that ambitious architects learn quickly. Any alteration in the balance of power between architect and client (author and reader) is likely to be strongly resisted. But, paradoxically, this is precisely what must happen if architects are to gain some influence over the design of ordinary, serially produced buildings like houses. Authorship must be shared with both the customer and the manufacturer. An architect submitting a design for a house to a manufacturer will be asked to alter *this* detail in order to make it easier to produce, and *that* detail in order to make it easier to sell. It will be an open collaboration, and the temptation to cry 'but this is no longer my design!' will have to be resisted. The only alternative is for architects to give up their ambitions to influence the everyday environment and go back to designing art galleries.

The birth of the reader must be at the cost of the death of the author. But what might 'the birth of the reader' mean in an architectural context? One thinks first of vernacular architecture. 'Vernacular' is, after all, a term borrowed from literature and linguistics. Vernacular architecture, the traditional Japanese house for example, is an architecture innocent of authorship and locked into tradition, the building equivalent of the old stories told by the shaman. Its characteristics – simplicity, anonymity, the repetition of standard components and types – sometimes seem very close to those of industrialized building. But the comparison shouldn't be pushed too far. When we use the word 'vernacular' we mean the pure, direct expression of a settled way of life, and nobody would describe modern industrial society in these terms. True vernacular architecture, like true Gothic architecture, is a lost and irrecoverable ideal. Industry can't do vernacular any more than architects can. So how will the architectural 'readership' assert itself? In what 'language' will it find meaning? The idea of architecture as language is an old one, most recently revived in the Postmodernism of the 1970s and '80s, since defeated within the profession by a resurgence of Modernism in various altered forms. But architectural theory cannot create a language. Language is by its very nature traditional, a thing given and shared, not invented. A language without a past has no meaning.

We don't have to look far for something resembling an architectural language because it is right there on every suburban residential street, despised and neglected by architects: the architecture of popular housing. In Britain, where private housing has traditionally been supplied on a speculative basis, where houses are joined together in pairs and rows, and where a house is expected to last a hundred years, the language of popular housing has a limited and static vocabulary. Consumers contribute little to it. But in the US, where to live in a detached house is almost regarded as a human right, where some families change houses as frequently as they change cars, and where a new house is a customized commodity, the architecture of popular housing is a living language. Like any language, its roots reach far back into history, beyond the twentieth century, beyond the Civil War, beyond the Revolution, back to the old countries. The 'Colonial' house – English, Dutch, Spanish or French – is still a recognizable prototype. When all the ungrammatical borrowings from other styles are removed from a typical suburban house, a basic Cape Cod (single-storey, side-gabled with rooms in the roof) or New England Salt Box (two-storey with a single-storey extension under the extended back roof slope) is often revealed. And these terms are still in use by pattern book authors and real estate agents. Occasionally you will come across a simple, tasteful restatement of one these prototypes – an elegant 'Williamsburg' colonial with three gabled dormers, or a plain Cape Cod with 'authentic' slightly bowed roof slopes – but mostly the modern suburban house is an eclectic mixture of features plundered from 350 years of architectural history. Over that period, certain styles have been recycled so many times that historians have run out of prefixes. A small house with a two-storey pedimented portico (a common sight) ought strictly to be called neo-neo-classical revival. English terms like Tudor, Georgian, Victorian and Queen Anne are still in use to designate certain features, although in American English they mean something slightly different. The Queen Anne style, for example, was originally inspired by the architecture of Norman Shaw and in its current manifestation would more commonly be

Colonial-style house, Oak Park, Chicago.

called 'Victorian', or possibly 'Neo-Victorian'. But not everything is adapted from the Old World. The Craftsman style, first promoted in the early 1900s by Gustav Stickley, publisher of the *Craftsman* magazine (see Chapter 5), and later associated with the 'bungalow craze' of the 1920s, still exerts an influence. Occasional inter-breedings with 'proper' architecture have also diversified the gene pool. Traces of Frank Lloyd Wright's Prairie Style or McKim, Mead & White's Shingle Style are still recognizable in certain individuals.

What Americans call the 'reminiscent' styles provide the basic vocabulary of the popular suburban house, but this doesn't mean that the language is stagnating. Stylistic features are constantly being reinterpreted and recombined to make new forms. Recently something called 'The Great Room' has made an appearance in place of the old living-room. It has a high ceiling, sometimes fully double height with a gallery. If the ceiling is especially elaborate it may be called a 'cathedral ceiling'; at the very least it will have a dished profile called a 'tray ceiling'. Where this new interest in height and ceilings comes from is a mystery; possibly it is a recollection of English medieval manor houses with minstrel galleries seen while on the grand tour of Europe. The 'breakfast nook' is another recent coinage, a new answer to the old problem of the relationship between kitchen, dining-room and living-room. Entrance halls have become 'foyers', not just circulation spaces but rooms in their own right, with perhaps a bay window or an alcove with a pair of columns in antis. These new forms, and new names, exist happily alongside the old. A specialist architectural term like 'Palladian window' will still be used perfectly correctly, although the window in question might be in a garage wall. 'Stucco', 'quoin', 'keystone', 'pilaster' – architectural terms like these have a certain cachet and can be dropped into the marketing blurb to flatter the customer. Eclecticism is now so radical that the old styles, the styles recognized by architectural history, are breaking up and difficult to pick out. But they are not dying, they are merely reconfiguring themselves under new headings: 'European', 'Mediterranean', 'Nostalgic', 'Country', 'Traditional'.

The language of popular housing may be vulgar and tasteless, but it is owned and used and understood by the population of suburban America in a way that proper architecture can only envy. Compared with this colourful montage of architectural memories, the architect-designed Modernist house, supposedly style-less and each one an original invention, as if nobody had ever designed a house before, seems a soulless thing to most people. It is hard for real architects to participate in the language of popular housing because the concept of authorship keeps getting in the way. Customers' requirements are expressed not in abstract, quasi-legal briefs but in traditional forms with established names – porches, dormers, bay windows, balconies, great rooms and cathedral ceilings. Nobody 'designed' these, they are just a part of the language. Composition is what is called for, not design.

Architects have long been aware of the gulf between popular taste and architectural taste and some have tried to bridge the gap by engaging with 'ordinary' building. For certain English architects, 'the ordinary' has become a kind of cult. The founders of this cult were Alison and Peter Smithson, who made their name in the early 1950s with the design of a now famous school at Hunstanton in Norfolk, an extremely austere steel-framed building later identified as the first example of the style known as New Brutalism. The Smithsons were founder members of an informal association of avant-garde artists called the Independent Group, which included the photographer Nigel Henderson, the sculptor Eduardo Paolozzi and the architecture critic Peter Reyner Banham. They put on exhibitions at the Institute of Contemporary Arts in London celebrating various aspects of ordinariness, from garden sheds to science fiction films. Paradoxically it was ordinariness – the bringing of ordinary things into the art gallery – that made the group special. In 1955 the engineer and acoustician Derek Sugden asked the Smithsons to design an 'ordinary' house for him and his wife on a suburban site in Watford, just north of London. Alison Smithson produced the first sketch scheme, with a butterfly roof and narrow windows. Sugden didn't like it and told her so, making her 'very cross'. Peter Smithson then produced another design that met with Sugden's full approval.[6]

The house is indeed ordinary: two-storey, with load-bearing walls of second-hand stock brick and a double pitched roof covered with cheap concrete tiles. Externally there are no modernist features and nothing that would upset the most conservative planning officer, except perhaps a slightly wrong-looking arrangement of standard steel-framed windows. Inside, there are

Sugden House by Alison and Peter Smithson.

Sugden House interior.

some more obviously architectural features such as fair-face brickwork, exposed timber floor joists and sloping ceilings over the upper floor, but these could hardly be described as extraordinary. And yet there *is* something extraordinary about the Sugden House. Perhaps it is those windows, arranged, no doubt, for optimum daylight and to take advantage of the views, but also with a kind of deliberate awkwardness, their heads sometimes lining up and sometimes not. Or perhaps it is the absence of any traditional decorative features like barge-boards or porches or coloured infill panels – the sort of thing that would be routine in a builder's version of the house.

It is not so much ordinary as an *exercise* in the ordinary. Ordinariness has become an architectural theme rather than a natural quality.

Forty years later, the Sugden house was to be influential on two closely related young practices, Caruso St John and Sergison Bates. Adam Caruso and Peter St John designed a house on the edge of a Lincolnshire village that, like the Sugden House, is two-storey and apparently built mainly of brickwork with a tile-covered pitched roof. According to the architects it 'vaguely resembles, on first appearance, the modern bungalows and detached houses that characterise the village'.[7] So from a distance it looks ordinary. Closer, however, it also turns out to be an enigmatic little building. The roof is ambiguous: asymmetrical, both hipped and gabled with each of the three slopes at a different pitch, making the house look single-storey from some viewpoints and two-storey from others. Windows, as in the Sugden House, are arranged according to a hidden logic, so that some look too small, others too big, and all lack conventional mullions and transoms. Even the reassuringly ordinary brickwork has been subtly manipulated to undermine expectations. There are no visible lintels over the openings (not in itself unusual, but a clear nod in the direction of Sugden) and the corners are trimmed with steel angles so that only the surface of the brickwork is visible, not its thickness. Inside we find a big double-height space, a kind of 'great room', overlooked not by a balcony but by a window in the wall of the master bedroom. The ceiling echoes the roof slopes, but not precisely because there is some quite hefty structure in between. A fireplace in the corner is placed right next to a nondescript little door, like the door of a cupboard, that opens onto the staircase. It is a fascinating, almost disturbing piece of domestic architecture and it certainly isn't ordinary.

Jonathan Sergison and Stephen Bates's homage to the Sugden House is less enigmatic. It is that typically English thing, a pair of two-storey semi-detached houses, and it is sited on an ordinary suburban housing estate in Stevenage. The design won a competition promoted by a housing association to celebrate its centenary. In view of these special circumstances, it is not surprising that the architects produced something out of the ordinary, but ordinariness is the theme, nevertheless. Two archetypal house forms, their gable ends facing the road, have been squashed together but at a slight angle so that they remain distinct forms. One might expect them to be 'identical-but-handed' in the normal way, but actually they have different plans (one has three bedrooms, the other two), different window patterns and differently coloured (grey and brown) cladding. The other unusual feature, and the one most commented on by non-architects, is the cladding of the roof and the upper parts of the walls in the same material – artificial slate – with no overhangs, fascias or barge-boards to mark the transition from roof to wall. It is as if the houses have been carved out

Semi-detached houses in Stevenage by Sergison Bates.

of a solid material, like the wooden houses on a Monopoly board. Expectations are thus undermined in several ways but these are still in some sense ordinary semi-detached houses. They are not new inventions. Their ordinary prototype is still recognizable and they would not make sense architecturally without it.

The Sugden House, the Lincolnshire House and the Stevenage houses – all are commentaries on the ordinary. There are extremely refined architectural sensibilities at work here, and ideas of a subtlety that only the most sophisticated client could possibly be interested in: ideas, for example, about the relationship between form and construction. In these buildings space and form take precedence over structure and construction. The brick walls of the Lincolnshire house are denied any opportunity to express their load-bearing function and the innovative composite timber-frame structure of the Stevenage houses is nowhere visible. This is the opposite of High Tech, of which it is implicitly critical. There are ideas too about emotional responses to buildings and places. This is Sergison Bates on the deeper intentions of their work:

> If acted upon consciously, within a conceptual framework, architecture may go beyond programme and site by engaging with personal and collective experience of place and our position in the world.

And further on:

> Embodying conceptual ideas in production with the objective of encouraging new ways to see the commonplace has been the concern of minimal and Pop art as well as socio-realist photography. The communicative nature of this work has drawn our attention.[8]

Ordinariness, in other words, has been appropriated by art, subtly altered and returned to the streets of the city. But perhaps the alteration is not as subtle as all that. The residents of a Lincolnshire village or a Stevenage housing estate may not be able to appreciate the conceptual niceties of these buildings, but one thing is clear to everyone: that they are the products of authorship. They might as well wear ten-foot-high sky signs saying 'Architect Designed'.

# 5. Professionalism and pattern books

Architecture is a fertile field for the cultivation of metaphor. The word 'architecture' itself makes frequent appearances outside its dictionary definition ('the art or science of constructing edifices for human use'), being applied to almost any large and complex structure, whether concrete or abstract – a novel, say, or a computer system. And of course the word 'architect' has even wider currency. In politics, for example, we speak of the architect of a foreign policy or of a grand alliance. Sometimes metaphorical architects are unfortunate ('he was the architect of his own downfall'), but mostly an architect is a good thing to be – creative, comprehending, skilful, reliable. Most famously and fundamentally, there is a long tradition of describing and depicting God as the architect of the universe.

Architecture commonly serves as a metaphor for thought itself. Descartes, in his *Discourse on Method*, writes about the philosophical system he is about to construct as if it were a project to rebuild his house:

> . . . it is not sufficient, before commencing to rebuild the house which we inhabit, to pull it down and provide materials and an architect (or to act in this capacity ourselves, and make a careful drawing of its design) unless we have also provided ourselves with some other house where we can be comfortably lodged during the time of rebuilding . . . I [therefore] formed for myself a code of morals for the time being . . .[1]

Note that the house can be both a philosophical and a moral construction, and that it is not a mere structure, but a dwelling place. The more you think about thinking, the more architectural it becomes. Arguments are constructed dialectically, like beams on columns, storey upon storey, strengthening and buttressing one another. If the thought-structure is not well founded then it will totter and collapse into ruins. Philosophy, like architecture, is hierarchical. It has its essential and its inessential parts, its axioms, its predicates and its rhetorical flourishes, its base, its superstructure and its ornament. But the architectural metaphor doesn't stand for just any kind of thought; it stands for organized, coherent, productive thought, the kind of thought that keeps a grip on reality and genuinely seeks truth.

Architectural metaphors almost always imply permanence and stability. Buildings are expected to endure and to stay put. In his essay 'Building, Dwelling, Thinking', Heidegger points out that the German word for building, *bauen*, comes from the Old German word *buan*, which means to dwell, to remain, to stay in one place.[2] To build is to make a place in which to dwell. And the first act of building, according to Heidegger, is the making of a clearing in the forest in which building and dwelling alike will be 'revealed'. Clearing, building, dwelling, thinking – all are combined, inseparably, in the 'thrownness of being'. Heidegger's clearing will surely contain a permanent settlement, and permanence has enormous ethical implications that are also locked into the language. 'Solid', 'established' and 'long-standing' shade into 'steadfast', 'constant' and 'true'. Architecture is therefore associated with all that is dependable and morally upright. Even 'morally upright' has architectural overtones. By our edifices are we edified. (Edify: to instruct, improve; to profit spiritually or mentally.)

In view of this, it is not surprising that traditional architectural theory should have taken on a strong moral character. The moral colours of the architectural metaphor are reflected back onto architecture itself. On the face of it, there is nothing intrinsically moral about the design of a building, apart from the ordinary ethical considerations that might apply to any social undertaking, yet architectural theorists have consistently tended to apply moral criteria to the judgment of otherwise practical matters like the arrangement of plans, the use of materials and the disposition of structure. The tendency is particularly marked among the Gothicists of the nineteenth century. In 'The Lamp of Truth', the second of *The Seven Lamps of Architecture*, for example, John Ruskin forbids any kind of deceit, such as 'the suggestion of a mode of support other than the true one', 'the painting of surfaces to represent some other material' and, interestingly, 'the use of cast or machine-made ornaments of any kind'.[3] Everything in a building must be 'honest'. Machine-made ornament is dishonest because the craftsmanship it displays is an illusion.

For Ruskin, truth to materials and the honest expression of structure or function were more notional than actual, part of architecture's wider responsibility to project a picture of a stable society. But the modernists of the twentieth century brought a new literal-mindedness to the moral structure of architecture. It was no longer enough just to keep ornament in its place; it had to be made a crime and banished completely, as it was from the exteriors of the

Gothic tracery from John Ruskin,
*Seven Lamps of Architecture*
(2nd edition, 1855).

proto-modernist houses of Adolf Loos. And it was no longer enough just to be conscious of the difference between structural and non-structural parts; the two had to be radically differentiated so that there could be no possible doubt about which was which. The steel frames and glass curtain walls of buildings by Mies van der Rohe come to mind.

Quite why an architectural theory associated with the nineteenth-century Gothic Revival should have remained so influential throughout the twentieth century is something of a mystery, especially since there were perfectly respectable and more interesting alternatives available to follow. The German architect Gottfried Semper, for example, constructed his theory along quite different lines. Rejecting a value-laden, hierarchical system in which the parts of a building that bear load are more important than those that merely divide space, Semper thought of architecture in terms of four basic industries – ceramics, masonry, carpentry and weaving – which found their own levels of importance in any given building according to social and geographical circumstances. In Semper's system, ornament is more important than structure, since it represents the essential cosmogonic or 'world creating' function of architecture.[4]

And if a form developed in one material (carved in wood, say) is reproduced in another (cast in iron, perhaps), then this is only the necessary deception that architecture has practised ever since a wooden temple was translated into stone in ancient Greece to inaugurate the whole classical tradition.

But it was the Ruskinian tradition that prevailed and set the moral tone for the twentieth century, a tone that to this day can be heard loud and clear wherever architects gather to discuss their craft. A morally good building is assumed to be: (1) permanent; (2) fixed in one place (built from the bottom up on firm foundations); (3) architect-designed; and (4) unique. If any item on this list remains unchecked, then the building in question will probably not qualify as 'proper' architecture. This prejudice is, as we have seen, locked into the language. But now let's consider the words that might be applied to the making of temporary, portable, anonymous or mass-produced buildings; words like 'fabricate', 'invent' and 'manufacture'. In *Roget's Thesaurus*, these three are followed, in the same paragraph, by: trump up, make up, get up, hatch, concoct, cook up, fudge up, fake up, hoke up, counterfeit and forge. Even a seemingly innocent word like 'assemble' has shady etymological connections with 'resemble', and thereby with 'dissemble' – to alter or disguise.

No wonder ordinary buildings like prefabricated houses have trouble being taken seriously by architects, historians and theorists. Take the balloon frame house, for example. To understand the theoretical significance of the balloon frame method of construction, it is necessary to understand what it superseded. The word 'frame' is commonly used to describe heavyweight structures in timber, steel or reinforced concrete that should more properly be called 'post-and-beam'. In post-and-beam structures, the original prototypes of which were the classical 'orders' of columns and entablatures, upright supports are widely spaced creating large openings. Where enclosure of space is required, non-load-bearing walls, usually relatively light and often divided into panels, are fixed into the openings. The Farnsworth House by Mies van der Rohe, with its steel frame and glass walls, is a good example. The hierarchical distinction between frame and infill is a common grammatical construction in the language of architecture. Traditionally, the alternative is to combine load-bearing and weather-protecting functions in a solid stone or brick wall. Openings are bridged either by lintels or, more purely, by arches made of similar stones or bricks. This construction principle originated in ancient Rome and reached its peak of development in the medieval Gothic that was so much admired by nineteenth-century theorists. Most western architecture can be fitted into one or other of these two traditions: post-and-beam or arcuated, Classical or Gothic.

Farnsworth House by Mies van der Rohe.

All Saints church, Burton Dassett, Warwickshire,
arcuated portal.

But the balloon frame fits neither. It is both a frame and a continuous wall. The vertical and horizontal members of the frame are too close together to be thought of as spatially open, too close even for a single door opening. To describe them as columns and beams would be absurd. And the 'siding' that keeps the weather out doesn't infill the frame but covers it like an overcoat, hiding it and therefore depriving it of any architectural, as opposed to structural, function. All you see is the linear texture of the clapboards, non-hierarchical, featureless, dumb. The balloon frame is an architectural contradiction in terms: light and thin but load-bearing, drawing its strength from the three-dimensional bracing effect of floors and roof. Each stud supports a joist, each joist braces a stud. As practical building construction it is brilliant; as traditional architecture, it is nowhere.

Moral ideas about truth to materials and honesty of expression are largely irrelevant to the balloon frame house. Structure is hidden and forms no part of the architecture, so it doesn't matter what the structure is made of or how it works. This doesn't mean, however, that the building's appearance is of no concern to its designers. On the contrary, architecture, in the narrow sense of image and surface appearance, will often be an essential marketing tool and a fundamental basis of classification and consumer choice. But the architecture will be applied, not intrinsic. It will be a 'false façade' (note the ethical overtones of that phrase). Almost as soon as it was invented, the

Wooden siding and applied architectural details on a Finnish house.

Classical portico under construction on a timber-framed American suburban house.

balloon frame was being used as an armature for an imitation architecture. Of all the styles that the early balloon framed buildings of Chicago could have chosen to dress themselves up in, the Greek Revival – solid and serious, the very essence of rectitude – seems the least appropriate. Yet little balloon-framed houses with pedimented porticos and big, showy cornices became almost universal in the Midwest of the 1840s and '50s. Later in the century, tastes changed and a riotous eclecticism ruled, combining Romanesque, Gothic, Italianate and Queen Anne, sometimes in the same house. But always behind the scenes it was a simple balloon frame that did all the structural work. It is still the same today.

Unique, site-specific buildings are favoured by architectural practice as well as architectural theory. There are many ways to practise architecture, but most of them are variations on a generally agreed norm. To practise architecture the normal way, an architect first has to find a client with money to spend and a site on which to build. Before any decisions can be made about the size and shape of the proposed new building it will be necessary to analyse the client's requirements and write them down in the form of a brief. This is supposed to be an objective, almost scientific document, free of 'preconceptions', such as what the new building might look like. The next task is to survey and analyse the site in a similarly objective way, measuring it in three dimensions and listing its qualities under headings such as aspect, prospect, orientation, bearing capacity of the soil and so on. When these tasks have been completed the architect goes away, usually for several weeks, and comes back with a sketch scheme in the form of a set of drawings: plans, sections, elevations and perhaps a perspective view. If the sketch scheme meets with the client's approval, then the architect goes away again and develops the design through various stages, such as obtaining town planning approval, finalizing the technical details and producing working drawings. Several builders are invited to tender for the job and a contract is signed between the client and lowest bidder. Construction then proceeds under the watchful eye of the architect who, in the case of any dispute, is supposed to act impartially between the client and the builder.

Normal practice in its pure form is becoming less common as new kinds of building contract are devised and new technologies such as computer-aided design are introduced. Nevertheless, it still effectively defines architecture as a profession. It assumes that architecture is a service, not a product; that buildings are purpose-made for specific clients and specific sites; that the designer and the client are known to one another; and that the architect is responsible for the technologies employed in the construction of the building as well as its overall form. Architectural education broadly supports these assumptions. An architect's training consists mainly of a sequence of design projects of increasing size and complexity that imitate normal practice. Teachers will often reinterpret normal practice in various ways in order to introduce certain philosophical ideas or emphasize certain skills. For example, it is common for the site analysis part of the process to be given prominence. Most college projects are designed for real sites and students will spend weeks observing, recording, analysing and 'mapping' whole tracts of the surrounding urban environment, developing a sensitivity to every nuance of its social and physical nature. Real clients are more difficult to obtain so they usually have to be invented, often complete with personal characteristics and life histories. Construction technology is typically given a lower priority than 'pure design', and money is almost never mentioned. All the same, if you examine the official course documents, you are sure to find a recognizable reflection of normal practice. In more progressive schools, the reinterpretations may be so radical that the reflection becomes grossly distorted. Technical design may be almost completely disregarded on the principle that knowledge of structures, construction and building services inhibits creativity. Sometimes even the very idea that architecture has something to do with the design of buildings may be called into question. Projects become rarefied and conceptual – installations, virtual environments, clothing, games – and there is much talk of 'art practice'. But when this happens, the profession usually intervenes through various course validation mechanisms and the school is advised to return to something closer to normal practice, with sites and clients and buildable buildings.

It is hard to make the assumptions of normal practice fit the design of prefabricated or serially produced buildings. In fact if we take popular housing as an example, the opposite assumptions would seem to be more appropriate. The idea of having to pay to have their requirements listed in a brief 'without preconceptions' is unlikely to be attractive to potential house buyers. They want to see the product before they commit themselves. Architects often argue that the site-specific nature of architecture makes buildings unsuitable subjects for serial production. There are a number of possible objections to this argument, the most obvious being that most buildings are serially produced and have been for many years. They may not have been made on factory production lines like cars, but most traditional English houses – the fourth-rate Georgian cottages of Islington, the Victorian terraced houses of a Lancashire mill town, the Tudor-gabled semis of Metroland – were essentially standard products, serially produced without any significant adjustments to fit particular sites. And of course the serially produced house, whether as a design or an actual building, is of necessity a speculative venture, an attempt to meet the needs not of an individual but of a market sector. A customer for a house may well have special requirements, but these will be accommodated by adaptations to a standard type and the designer of that type will probably no longer be involved. Designer and client do not usually meet.

Finally, the assumption of normal architectural practice that the same designer should be responsible for the technology of the building as well as its formal and spatial characteristics is highly questionable as far as serial production is concerned. Spatial design and technical design are sometimes closely related (indeed a belief in the closeness of that relationship is one of the cornerstones of Modernist architectural theory), but they nevertheless require different skills. The efficient serial production of houses depends on commercial as well as technical factors. A change in the market price of certain materials might suggest a radical change in the design of the product, for example from load-bearing brickwork to timber frame, and this change might have little effect on the overall form of the building. The spatial designer is not necessarily the person best qualified to take such decisions. Neither is he or she in a good position to assess the technical design consequences of, say, the arrival of a new machine in the workshop, or of a new production manager with new ideas. The slow but sure industrialization of the whole building industry, not just the housing industry, is making architects' claims to be in charge of technical as well as spatial design less and less credible. It doesn't mean that architects couldn't be good factory-based technical designers: they could, but it would involve a shift in their self-image, in particular the image of themselves as independent, disinterested professionals, which is another of the doubtful assumptions of 'normal practice'.

So how might normal practice adapt to the demands of a new factory-based and market-orientated building industry? One way might be simply to change the order in which things are done by designing the building first and consulting the client later. This is anathema to most modern architects, who become active only when someone brings them a problem to solve. Architectural practices with too little work to do will often keep busy by entering architectural competitions, because this provides them with what they regard as the essential preconditions of architecture: a brief and a site. Their time might be better spent designing buildings for which they know there is a demand, like houses, schools, medical centres or retail outlets, and publishing the designs. But there seems to be a general resistance among architects to this rather obvious ploy. Partly it is a hangover from the days when their professional code forbade all sorts of normal commercial activities like advertising. It might also have something to do with the question of authorship (see Chapter 4) and the insistence that money should change hands before a design is made public. But mostly it is a reluctance to let go of the idea that a building must be designed for a particular site. Behind this idea lies that strange, largely unexamined, assumption that every building, certainly every architect-designed building, should ideally be unique, because every site is unique. The building becomes the expression of the uniqueness of the site. Through architecture, the site becomes more than a site; it becomes a 'place'. In other words architecture, in its fundamental nature, is site specific.

If this were really the case, then architecture and serial production would never be reconciled. But history would seem to indicate that this insistence on uniqueness is an aberration rather than an essential quality of architecture. Vernacular architecture, so much admired by modern architects for its purity and rightness in the landscape, always consists of a relatively small number of standard building types: the cottage, the manor house, the barn, the parish church. Every medieval English parish church is in a sense unique, but equally the great majority are composed from a limited repertoire of standard components (nave, chancel, tower, porch) and standard decorative schemes (Early English, Decorated, Perpendicular) developed over centuries to suit common conditions, not specific sites. The permutations may be infinite, creating an endlessly fascinating richness, but the basic components are standard. The history of architecture is the history of the adaptation and recombination of established types and styles. And if modernist architects insist on throwing out tradition, the results still only makes sense as rejections of tradition.

Architects' resistance to the idea of designing buildings speculatively and without reference to any specific site is all the more surprising when you realize that this was a perfectly normal part of architectural practice before the twentieth century. Collections of speculative designs were published in pattern books, which served as guides for clients and builders, and advertisements for architects. 'Pattern book' has now become shorthand for all that is shoddy and careless in the design of buildings. Architects pour scorn on pattern books. But there was a time when the pattern book was, so to speak, where architecture resided.

In Elizabethan England the word 'architecture' was hardly ever used (you won't find it anywhere in the complete works of Shakespeare) and there were no professional architects in the modern sense. People who 'designed' buildings called themselves masons, carpenters or artificers. Designing a building was a collaborative process and it was almost unknown for a single author to be identified. Robert Smythson's epitaph in Wollaton church reads 'Architecter and Survayor unto the most worthy house of Wollaton with divers others of great account', but according to John Summerson this precise evidence of authorship is 'a case almost unique in Elizabethan architecture'.[5] A client for a large-scale building project like a country house might invite one mason to draw the plan, another to draw the elevations and yet another to employ the workmen and supervise operations on site. Ornamental set pieces like porches, staircases and fireplaces would be commissioned from individual craftsmen who would often adapt designs published in books. It was through these books, directly or indirectly, that the new classical style of ornament, based on ancient Roman architecture, filtered into the country from Italy via France, Flanders and Germany. Whenever the word architecture was used, it was in reference to this new style. Architecture basically meant designs published in pattern books.

For 300 years the pattern book remained the chief medium by which respectable architecture was disseminated in England. Sixteenth-century Italian originals, such as the six books of Sebastiano Serlio's treatise and Andrea Palladio's *I quattro libri dell'architettura*, inspired countless imitations, from John Shute's *First and Chief Groundes of Architecture* of 1563 to the lavish publications of the eighteenth century, such as Colen Campbell's *Vitruvius Britannicus* (1715–25) and James Gibbs's *A Book of Architecture* (1728). The builders of the elegant streets and squares of Georgian London took their

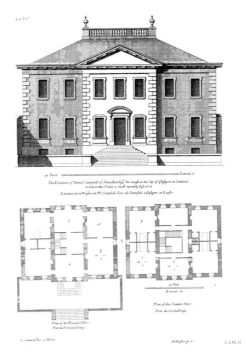

Plate from Colen Campbell's
*Vitruvius Britannicus.*

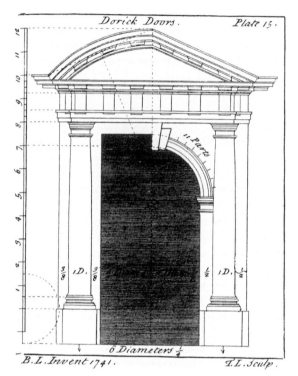

correctly proportioned façades and Doric door-cases straight from smaller, cheaper pattern books such as William Halfpenny's *The Art of Sound Building* (1725) and Batty Langley's *The Builder's Jewel* (1741). In the early nineteenth century dozens of architects produced pattern books to meet the demand from a growing middle class for suburban villas and country cottages. One of the pioneers of the so-called 'villa book' was Sir John Soane, architect of the Bank of England and often regarded as the first truly professional architect in the modern sense. His *Sketches in Architecture* of 1793 is purely speculative, containing designs for modest, affordable dwellings pictured in imaginary rural settings.

By the mid-nineteenth century in England the pattern book was being eclipsed by the rise of the architectural magazine. In the USA, however, it was spreading and beginning to mutate in interesting ways. Andrew Jackson Downing published *Cottage Residences* in 1842 and *The Architecture of Country Houses* in 1850. These enormously popular books contained designs for mainly Italianate and Gothic Revival houses, based on the new 'balloon frame' method of timber construction. Dozens of imitations appeared over the next twenty years. In 1876 George Palliser, an English immigrant who had worked as a carpenter and joinery manufacturer, published a 25 cent booklet called *Model Homes for the People*. It was the first of 21 pattern books to be produced by Palliser and his brother Charles over the next twenty years. The Pallisers marketed themselves as architects and used their pattern books not simply as advertisements for their practice but much more actively as lures to catch clients. The potential client would choose a design from one of the books, then write to the practice describing any alterations that might be required. The practice would send a sketch for approval before producing a full set of plans, elevations, sections, details and specifications to be used as tender documents by local carpenters. The Pallisers were not the first firm to offer blueprints by mail-order, by they were the first to turn the process into a kind of architectural consultancy based on the adaptation of standard designs.

There was an educational element in the American pattern book, though it was sometimes corrupted by underlying commercial motives. The eclectic Victorian designs, all turrets, gables and porches, encrusted with finials and flummery, would hardly be called tasteful now, and it has been argued that the designs were made deliberately complicated in order to convince customers of the need to buy the blueprints. Nevertheless the pattern book was seen as the means of bringing architecture to the masses and beauty to the cities and suburbs. Gustav Stickley, the editor of a monthly magazine called *The Craftsman*, founded in 1903, set out to cleanse the American architectural palate by promoting a new, simple Arts and Crafts influenced style. Naturally, he published pattern books to make the new style accessible and usable by clients and builders. *More Craftsman Homes*, published in 1912, contains plans and views of 78 so-called 'mission style' houses and bungalows, each accompanied by a long descriptive text written with a care and attention to detail quite unlike the usual advertising blurb. The plans are relaxed and open, designed as spatial sequences rather than clusters of boxes. Many of the views are interiors, sensitively drawn, focusing on characteristic details – an inglenook fireplace, a window seat, the plain wooden beams of a living-room ceiling. Stickley overstretched himself and his business collapsed in 1916 but the Craftsman style lived on to become one of the many disparate ingredients of the American suburban vernacular.

One of the ways pattern book publishers made their money was by including advertisements for building products like boilers, ironmongery and sanitary ware. The next logical step was to supply the actual products. In 1900 the Gordon van Tine Company of Davenport, Iowa, began to supply components like doors, windows and staircases with their blueprints. Very soon, other companies like the Aladdin Company of Bay City, Michigan, and, most

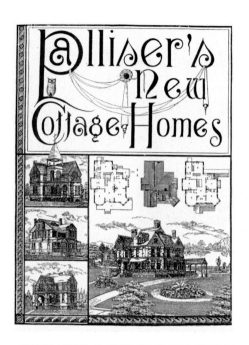

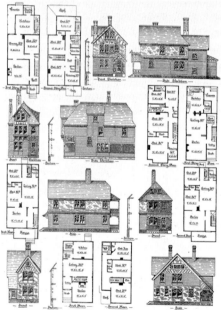

Frontispiece from Palliser's
*New Cottage Homes.*

Page from Palliser's
*New Cottage Homes.*

Illustration from Gustav Stickley's *More Craftsman Homes.*

famously, Sears Roebuck of Newark, New Jersey, were supplying complete pre-fabricated houses by mail order (see Chapter 2).

The mail-order house business did not survive the Wall Street crash of 1929, but the basic pattern book method pioneered by the Palliser brothers survives to this day. In Britain, where most new housing is provided by speculative developers, the pattern book is no longer a familiar medium, although demand is growing as the 'self-build' market gains ground. This demand is met mainly by package-build companies and by imports from America. In America, pattern books are as common as women's magazines. Whole shelves are filled with them in bookstores, supermarkets, motel receptions and airport lounges. Some are merely free brochures distributed by local builders with a credit 'pre-qualification' form to fill in on the back. Others are fat paperbacks, costing $10 or so, often compilations from a variety of sources, published in association with home-making magazines. There are pattern books to suit all tastes (except perhaps 'good taste'), all pockets and all settings: *The Craftsman Collection, 200 Budget-Smart Home Plans, European Dream Homes, Hillside Homes, 1001 All Time Best Selling Home Plans*, and so on, and on – hundreds of books, thousands of designs. Domestic architecture in America is plentiful and cheap. Most pattern books follow the standard format: one house per page, with a plan, a view and a list of features including square footage. There are far too many house types to give them individual names, so they are

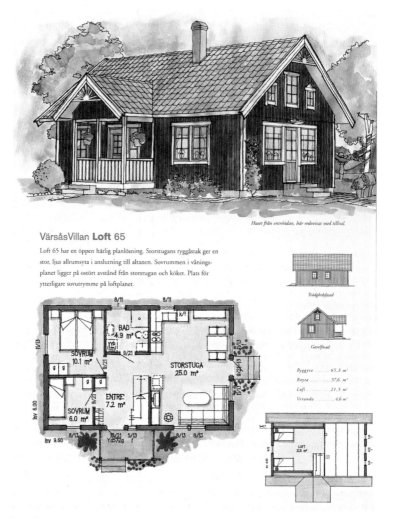

Page from a typical Swedish pattern-book.

designated by little descriptive phrases such as 'Charming with Drama', 'Captivating Colonial' and 'Balcony Offers Sweeping Views'. Each has a code number so that you can look up the cost of the blueprints. Typically, for about $700 you can get an eight-sheet package for a two-bed, two-bath 'Cape Cod'. For about twice that price the drawings will be supplied in CAD form on a CD-ROM. As well as a full set of working drawings, the package will include a list of materials, often with prices, an outline specification and various extras like room planning kits or information sheets about plumbing and electrical installations so that the customer can keep an eye on the builder.

Designs for pattern books are occasionally produced by fully qualified architects but more often by 'architectural design' practices. Authorship is hardly ever a selling point, although designers are sometimes credited. Despite the enormous variety of plans available, customizing is normal practice and pattern book companies are happy to cater for it. For an additional fee, in-house designers will carry out modifications based on the customer's sketches or, alternatively, drawings can be supplied in reproducible form for alteration by customers and their builders. Pattern book designs are always regarded as provisional. A customer finds the plan that comes nearest to meeting his or her requirements and then refines it. The refinements might be either spatial or stylistic, but they are unlikely to involve any fundamental change to the method of construction because the vast majority of pattern book house designs take for granted the 'platform frame' method (a development of the balloon frame) that has been standard throughout the US for 50 years. Blueprints don't normally include full framing plans, though they can be supplied for an extra charge, because it is assumed that a competent builder will be able to make that kind of detailed design decision on site. In Britain, pattern books are most often produced by package-build companies using prefabricated timber-frame systems. But timber frame is not the standard method of domestic construction in Britain, where load-bearing brick predominates, so house designs tend to remain tied to specific building companies. In the US the pattern book is free of specific allegiances because building technology is, as it were, already taken care of.

The main function of the American pattern book is to make sure individual customers get exactly what they want. But the pattern book can also be a means of controlling development. For example, it is an important weapon in the armoury of the movement known as New Urbanism, which fights back against suburban sprawl by reviving traditional urban forms. Planned communities like Seaside on the Florida Panhandle coast and Celebration, built by the Disney Corporation near the main gate of Disneyworld in Orlando, present themselves as new and different precisely because they are *not* gated communities. Celebration tries to recapture the spirit of the traditional American small town by a slight increase in planning density and innovations such as sidewalks, on-street parking, and a small downtown area in which shops and cafes front onto ordinary streets. Residents are actually encouraged to walk from their houses to the shops, a concept some find hard to grasp. Public buildings by famous architects are an added attraction: a cinema by Cesar Pelli, a bank by Robert Venturi and Denise Scott Brown, a town hall by Philip Johnson, a post office by Michael Graves. The architects' signatures are more important than the actual functions of the buildings. Seaside, master-planned by committed New Urbanists Andres Duany and Elizabeth Plater-Zyberk, became famous in Britain when the Prince of Wales and his architectural adviser, Leon Krier, gave it their seal of approval. Here too 'architecture' might be said to be the theme of the development, but with an added sophistication. Houses are generally classical, with many an elegant portico and belvedere, more correct and better proportioned than the usual pattern book versions of the style. Walking is encouraged here too, although tricycles and golf carts are popular.

At both Celebration and Seaside the pattern book technique has been used not to widen choice but to limit it. Urban Design Associates' Celebration pattern book is a complex document combining architectural styles and house types in a permutation matrix. There are six basic styles: Classical, Victorian, Colonial Revival, Coastal, Mediterranean and French. Each is considered in detail under six headings: History and Character, Massing, Porches, Doors and Windows, and Materials and Possibilities. The styles are then applied to

Typical Seaside house.

Seaside town centre.

a range of house types suitable for different neighbourhoods: Estate, Village, Cottage, Townhouse, Bungalow and Terrace. 'Landscape requirements', 'community patterns' and 'house placement criteria' complete the picture. According to its authors, the pattern book is a 'kit of parts that can be used by individual designers to create a wide range of houses while maintaining the character of traditional neighbourhood design'. To European eyes the result looks like standard suburbia with some bizarre touches, like the piped music that trickles constantly out of the undergrowth and the fact that dormer windows are always fake. But this doesn't invalidate the pattern book method, which avoids the tyranny of single authorship and makes use of the popular language of American domestic architecture to allow individual builders and house buyers a degree of choice (see Chapter 4).

It was historical accident – the Disney and Prince of Wales connections – that made Celebration and Seaside famous, but there are many similar developments all over the state, both gated and ungated, each with its unique selling points. An hour's drive north of Celebration, off Interstate 4 near DeLand, lies Victoria Park, a 1,859-acre (752-hectare) 'mixed-use' community divided into separate zones for different markets. Victoria Gardens is gated, with a private club featuring sports facilities, a ballroom and a business resource centre; Victoria Commons is the 'social centrepiece' of the development, with shops, some 'professional' offices and a recreation centre; Victoria Hills is a kind of inhabited golf course, the streets weaving between the fairways; and Victoria Farms is centred on the Freedom Elementary School. When complete, Victoria Park will accommodate more than 4,000 homes. The developers have employed an Art of Living Director to encourage social and cultural activities among the residents. The local newsletter is called *The Picket*

Celebration street scene. The dormer windows are always fake.

Celebration is no different from dozens of other Florida communities.

Typical pattern-book house at Celebration.

*Fence.* 'There used to be places like this', says one of the many glossy brochures, 'before the world got so busy and forgot the little things, like the necessity of a shady tree on a hot summer day, or the brilliance of a starry sky.' In reality it's just suburbia again, exclusive, secure and, like Celebration and Seaside, pattern book controlled.

But these communities are special applications of the pattern book principle. To see the pattern book in its natural habitat, wild and free, we must go hunting on the Web. The Internet is the perfect medium for the dissemination of domestic design. Many pattern book companies now have big websites offering thousands of house plans stored on databases searchable by type, style, square footage, average cost, number of bedrooms and so on. On a typical site, such as www.eplans.com, a search for a Colonial-style three-bedroom house to cost between $200,000 and $250,000 calls up 47 different designs. You can browse through them in summary form, enlarge the plans you like and save them to your hard drive, or alternatively fill out a registration form so that you can store them in a 'my plans' area. Photographic virtual tours are available for some designs, and there is often a customization gimmick, such as an elevation drawing on which you can try out different colours and finishes.

But computers have made possible a more radical way to involve customers in the design of their houses. The more adventurous and creative among them might like to try one of the many easy-to-use consumer CAD programs. Professional computer-aided design programs are too abstract and complex for ordinary house buyers to bother with, but the consumer versions, which restrict choice to a range of common forms, construction methods and materials, are manageable by any moderately computer-literate person. In 3D Home Architect, for example, you can start a design from scratch with a bubble diagram, roughly to scale. When you are happy with this, the program will convert it into a real plan and then offer a variety of roof forms, window and door types, siding materials, and additional features like porches and garden walls. When the design is finished, the program will automatically generate a framing plan and a list of materials so that, in theory at least, tenders could be obtained from builders. And everything, including the framing, is viewable in three dimensions from every angle. It would be difficult to design a really innovative house on this software. Assumptions are made and choices are restricted, but no more so that in pattern books. And of course many sample designs are included in the package. Most users will simply take one of these and adapt it, just as they would a pattern book design, leaving the bubble diagram method for purists and aspiring architects.

Pattern books can be used in many different ways. They can be mere sketchbooks to inspire potential customers or they can be mail-order catalogues

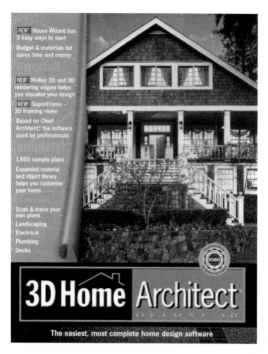

NEW! House Wizard has 3 easy ways to start

Budget & materials list saves time and money

NEW! Hi-Res 2D and 3D rendering engine helps you visualise your design

NEW! SuperFrame – 3D framing views

Based on Chief Architect, the software used by professionals

1,650 sample plans

Expanded material and object library helps you customise your home

Scan & trace your own plans
Landscaping
Electrical
Plumbing
Decks

**3D Home Architect**
DELUXE 4.0

The easiest, most complete home design software

Consumer CAD software.

to sell full sets of working drawings. The designs they contain can be either speculative or already executed, offered either as standard products or as starting points for a customization process. They can be tied to a specific method of construction, such as a proprietary timber-frame system, or they can be independent of any construction company, relying on local building traditions. They can be the product of a single author, and perhaps marketed as such, or they can be the result of collaboration between a spatial designer and a factory-based technical designer. Pattern books can be published in bulk to be sold in newsagents, or in limited editions targeted at specific clients. Or they can simply be published on the Internet. We think of pattern books mostly in connection with houses, but there is no reason why other common building types should not submit to the pattern book principle. George Palliser's first pattern book contained designs for a county bank, a library, a town hall, a masonic association building and several churches of different denominations.

Pattern books could be used to promote the sale of certain commercial products, but more importantly, they could also be used to promote good architecture and sound, sustainable building practices. There is no reason why the pattern book should be seen as a threat to 'real' architecture. It could be architecture's ally. As we have seen, it not only has a perfectly respectable history but in the past it has been an important medium for the growth and stabilization of the discipline and profession of architecture itself. It seems completely feasible for architects to adopt, or readopt, the pattern book principle. It may even be an essential precondition for the achievement of that century-old ambition to bring architecture to the masses. If architects are serious about this ambition, they should think again about their 'normal practice' and start publishing pattern books.

# 6. Down with the system

Regularity, rectilinearity, repetition, symmetry, geometrical coherence, articulation, hierarchy: these are qualities we usually associate with architecture. There are some exceptions, but normally we expect floors to be level, walls to be vertical, corners to be right angles, and columns to be similar to one another and regularly spaced. It might be the classical tradition, inaugurated by the temples of ancient Greece and still a constant reference point of western architecture, that gives rise to this expectation. But then regularity seems to be equally characteristic of non-western architectures, from mud huts to Indian temples.

Sometimes the regularity of architecture is taken to be the expression of a bigger idea, beyond the practicalities of building. The architects of the early Italian Renaissance, for example, were very interested in the idea of a consonance between architecture and music. The simple proportions displayed in their buildings – 1:2, 2:3, 3:4 – were called 'harmonic' because they were the geometrical equivalents of musical harmonies. If you pluck an open string on a guitar, then stop it exactly half way along its length (at the twelfth fret) and pluck it again, the interval you will hear is an octave. A rectangle with sides proportioned 1:2 (a double square, in other words) therefore represents the harmony of an octave. Similarly, the ratio 2:3 represents a perfect fifth, and 3:4 a fourth. So if the proportions of Brunelleschi's scheme for the church of San Lorenzo in Florence seem generally 'harmonious', it is because that is exactly what they are. The building is a kind of symphony.

But behind the idea that architecture could be, almost literally, harmonious, lies an even bigger idea. To the Renaissance mind, musical harmony was mysterious and magical. Its sweetness seemed like a small sample of the ultimate good, the harmony of the universe. And because the mathematical perfection of musical harmony was audible to everyone and immediately distinguishable from discord without the need for any measurement, humankind

Interior of San Lorenzo, Florence, by Brunelleschi.

was proved to be a part of this universal harmony. A harmonious building, therefore, had a cosmic significance.

In the modern age, the idea of the cosmic significance of simple ratios no longer holds sway but the general idea of geometrical coherence lives on both as an aesthetic ideal and as a practical measurement system to help with the complicated task of putting buildings together. By the beginning of the twentieth century geometry in architecture had lost its magic and become a mere tool. Here is Walter Gropius writing in 1910 about the possibilities for the industrialized production of houses:

> For all essential parts the best dimensions have to be decided first of all. These standard dimensions form the basis for the designs and are to be kept in future designs. Only by this means can mass sales be guaranteed and special making in the case of replacements and repairs be avoided.

Here geometry and proportion have been reduced to mere standardization. The dimensions of San Lorenzo were standardized too, but whereas the motive then was religious and philosophical, for Gropius it is purely practical: to avoid 'special making'.

The quotation comes from a long memorandum addressed to the management of the AEG electrical company and headed 'Programme for the Establishment of a Company for the Provision of Housing on Aesthetically Consistent Principles'.[1] In it, Gropius sets out, systematically and with remarkable prescience, what were to become the major themes in the architecture of prefabricated houses throughout the twentieth century. Most are still relevant today. He is aware, for example, of the importance of vernacular precedents, basing his designs on 'tested traditions, old as well as current'. He is anxious not to impose a dull uniformity and to allow a degree of what we would now call customization: 'The client can compose his house . . . according to his personal taste.' He knows that the product must be made visible to the public in 'well-designed leaflets illustrating and describing the various types of houses' - pattern books, in other words. He even proposes a form of what would now be called supply chain management: 'Contracts with suitable specialist manufacturers ensure that all parts satisfy the standards laid down by the company and are, if possible, permanently in stock.' He has no time for the sentimental idea that every building should be designed for a specific site: 'The houses . . . are independent, coherent organisms, not tied to any site.'

But the main theme of the memorandum is mass production. 'The idea of industrialization in housing can be translated into reality by repeating individual parts in all the designs promoted by the company. This makes mass production possible and promotes low costs and high rentability.' What he is proposing, then, is not a single house type, or even a family of standard types, but a system of components that can be combined in different ways to meet the special requirements of individual customers. Since the components are all to be designed and produced by a single company, it is what is usually called a 'closed' system. In order to make such a system work, the components – walls, ceilings, doors, windows – must all fit together fairly accurately, and this calls for some kind of dimensional coordination. A set of standard proportions might work very well: 1:2, 2:3 and 3:4, for example.

Gropius's proposal was very advanced for its time. Bear in mind that Henry Ford did not set up his first moving assembly line until three years later, in 1913, and that was for the production of a single type of car (the Model T) with, famously, no opportunities for customization. But Henry Ford's major innovation was not the moving assembly line, as is usually assumed. Sigfried Geidion pointed out many years ago that the first assembly lines were probably the 'disassembly lines' set up in the slaughterhouses of Cincinnati and Chicago in the

Ford assembly line,
Highland Park, 1914.

1850s.[2] The most important innovation in Ford's factory, and the one on which all the other short cuts and streamlinings depended, was the introduction of an unprecedented degree of dimensional accuracy in the production of hardened steel components. Previously components had been made or adjusted by hand for each individual car. This was the only way that the necessary accuracy of fit could be achieved. Ford saw that if the components could be made to an accurate standard gauge, they could be produced in quantity in the sure knowledge that they would fit any car. In other words they would be interchangeable. The general principle of interchangeability of components was not new. It had been developed in various industries such as gun-, clock- and lock-making in America by pioneers like Eli Whitney and Henry Maudslay, and had come to be known as the American System of Manufacture. But Ford was the first to apply it to hardened steel components, using new types of machine tool, and to make it the ruling principle for the production of complex engineering artefacts like cars.

Gropius was evidently well aware of the principle of interchangeable parts. It is one of the cornerstones of his proposal. But whereas for Henry Ford it was the key to the streamlining of production, for Gropius it was mainly a way to offer the customer variety and choice: 'It is by the provision of interchangeable parts that the company can meet the public's desire for individuality and offer the client the pleasure of personal choice and initiative without jettisoning aesthetic unity.' Gropius was an architect, not an engineer, and 'aesthetic unity' was more important to him than efficient production. This confusion of productive and aesthetic aims has characterized Modernism's engagement with industrial production ever since. Is the geometrical coherence of most

Modernist buildings fundamentally aesthetic or fundamentally productive? Which came first? It is impossible to say.

Gropius's proposal to AEG was not acted upon but his ideas gained currency through the Bauhaus design school in which, as director from 1919 to 1928, he maintained an unsteady balance between craft and industry. Instead of setting up a company to make and market houses, he set up a school to make and market ideas. Geometrical coherence, standard dimensions and the interchangeability of parts developed into a kind of ideological complex with practical, aesthetic and even moral aspects. And these ideas soon began to influence the progressive European architecture of the 1920s, such as the modernist housing schemes around Frankfurt designed under the leadership of Ernst May.

In America, too, the idea grew that the building process, in the factory and on the site, could be made more efficient by standardizing dimensions. In a three-volume book called *The Evolving House*,[3] Alfred Farwell Bemis directly compared the production of houses with the production of cars. It was not the first time that the question had been asked: why can't houses be made the way cars are made? But in his attempt to push house production closer to car production, Bemis introduced a new concept: modular coordination. (The use of the word 'modular' in this context, meaning based on a standard dimension, should not be confused with the later use of the word to describe a building made of prefabricated, room-size boxes.) The word 'module' comes from the Latin *modulus*, meaning a small measure. Bemis's module was a 4 in (100 mm ) cube. His idea was that all building components should be made in sizes that were multiples of the module. That way a perfect fit between components could be guaranteed and manufacturers could mass-produce and stockpile their products in the sure knowledge that they would find a market. A building would be designed as an abstract, three-dimensional matrix into which a range of interchangeable modular components could be inserted. Bemis illustrates this progression from abstract to real in clear isometric line drawings. The idea of modular co-ordination was to exert a powerful influence on industrially inclined architects for at least the next 40 years.

In fact, however, Bemis's four-inch module was little more than a systematization of traditional American domestic construction. In the 1940s and '50s institutions like the National Association of House Builders and the National Lumber Manufacturers' Association encouraged a simple, practical kind of modular co-ordination that was widely adopted by small builders and large developers alike. Most famous among the latter was William Levitt, whose development of 17,000 houses at Hempstead in Long Island came to be known as 'Levittown'. Levitt described his company as 'The General

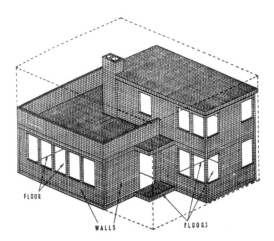

Bemis's module diagram.

Levittown from the air.

Motors of the Housing Industry'. His method was to clear a huge tract of land of every obstruction, including trees, and erect standard, detached 'Cape Cod' and 'Ranch Style' houses at regular intervals along straight roads on an assembly line basis. The construction sequence was divided into 26 steps and components such as pre-cut timber, staircases and kitchen cupboards were supplied from a central warehouse. Levitt claimed to build a new house every fifteen minutes, all with bathrooms and fitted kitchens, and many with built-in televisions.

In Europe, and especially in Britain, modular co-ordination had a rather different flavour. Among socially minded architects designing houses, schools and hospitals for the British welfare state after the Second World War, modular co-ordination was seen not just as a commonsense expedient but as an essential precondition for the industrial production of buildings. Hertfordshire County Council took the lead with a school-building programme based on the bulk purchase of standard lightweight steel and concrete components to be assembled on co-ordinating grids. The Hertfordshire schools claim a rightful place in architectural history for two reasons: in their lightness and simplicity they presented a pleasing image of a possible future factory-made Modernism, and their designers were genuinely committed to the ethical practice of architecture as a public service. In Andrew Saint's words, 'they wanted to build for the many, not for the few, and to do so co-operatively, modestly, justly and efficiently'.[4]

Building efficiently in the 1950s inevitably meant prefabrication, which in turn meant standardization and modular co-ordination. Various grid dimen-

Burleigh School,
Cheshunt, 1947.

Monkfirth School,
Barnet, 1950.

sions were tried out. A rather coarse 8 ft 3 in (2.5 metres), designed to suit the government's standard 24 ft (7.3 metre) wide classroom, was soon superseded by a more flexible 3 ft 4 in – ten of Bemis's four-inch modules and almost exactly one metre. Once fully committed to modular co-ordination, Hertfordshire began building schools at a fairly rapid rate: 91 primary schools were built in the county between 1945 and 1955. The government was impressed and soon modular co-ordination became official policy for school building, encouraged in Building Bulletins issued by the Ministry of Education. In 1953 the Modular Society was founded to promote the idea further and, as it were, to co-ordinate the co-ordination. Not surprisingly, it recommended a basic module of four inches. Other local authorities followed Hertfordshire's lead, forming consortia to develop new building systems for schools and other small public buildings. The Consortium of Local Authorities Special Programme (CLASP), set up in 1957, and the Second Consortium of Local Authorities (SCOLA), set up in 1961, were the most successful. They were, strictly speaking, closed systems, but both used 3 ft 4 in planning grids.

Modular Society
exhibition stand,
1958.

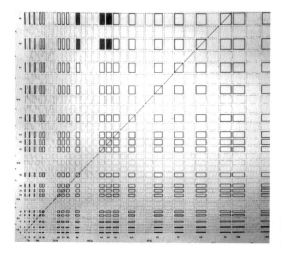

Building Research Establishment module chart, 1960.

By the mid-1960s, modular co-ordination was beginning to develop a degree of refinement and complexity quite foreign to the relatively crude technologies of building. The basic aim had always been to encourage the mass production of standard components that could be stockpiled for use in a rolling building programme. But now actual productive advantage began to seem less important than the internal logic of the modular system itself. Distinctions began to be made between different kinds of grids: structural grids, reference grids, planning grids, centre line, face-planned and tartan grids. Grids had become geometrical puzzles to be solved by the architect working at his drawing board, remote from any site or factory. The object of the game was to create the perfectly co-ordinated building, a three-dimensional nest of imaginary slots into which standard components would slide like Chippendale drawers. But real construction is not like that. In practice quite generous tolerances, or margins of error, have to be allowed. Tolerances have a habit of accumulating and getting out of control, so they had to be tamed, regulated and written into the rules of the game. Whole hierarchies of allowable variations were tabulated and whole glossaries of new terms invented: 'modular plane', 'modular space', 'modular size', 'work size', 'co-ordinating dimension' and so on.

Modular co-ordination had become a science. And still its ambitions grew. The idea now was not just to develop systems suitable for specific building types – schools or houses or hospitals – but to invent a system applicable to all building types: an 'open' system. This would be the interchangeability of parts taken to its logical conclusion; and it would be applied not just nationally, but across Europe. As early as 1956 the Organization for European Economic Co-operation published a report called 'Modular Co-ordination in Building'. After stating, as if it were an undisputed fact, that industrialized production methods were 'the only solution' for housing in Europe, it continues: 'One fundamental condition for such industrialized building production is the adoption of a modular system as a basis for standardization of building components.'[5]

The truth was, however, that far from being a fundamental condition for industrialized building, modular co-ordination was a deeply flawed conception based on a misunderstanding of the nature of manufacturing industry and an over-optimistic assessment of the achievable accuracy of building construction. Produced mainly by architects, it was a piece of abstract, conceptual architecture, and like much architecture it contained a large element of fiction. It told a story about production and construction, but the world it represented did not actually exist and the powers that it claimed were fantasies. It had all started with that perennial and provocative question: why can't we make buildings the way we make cars? The image of Henry Ford's Highland Park plant, a huge machine spewing out tens of thousands of cars a year, had inspired the idea of industrial building production and set designers off on a futile quest for the perfect system. But there had been a fundamental misunderstanding right from the start. Modular co-ordination had been based on the idea of the interchangeability of parts, which had been the key to the American System of Manufacture and, later, Ford's system of mass production. But in gun, clock, lock and car production, the interchangeability of parts meant the interchangeability of *identical* parts. What modular co-ordination tried to do was apply the principle to a variety of *different* parts, with different functions – doors, windows, wall panels etc. This was an interesting idea, and one which, as we shall see, may yet be relevant in the modern world of customization, but it had nothing to do with the practicalities of mass-production.

In the attempt to make a system of interchangeable different components work and apply that system on a limitless scale, modular co-ordination lost its grip on reality. Real mass production industries had never attempted any such thing. The idea of an open system would have seemed to them a nightmare. As Chris Abel pointed out as long ago as 1969, taken to its logical conclusion the open system idea implied that 'no component could be seriously modified unless like changes were performed on all other related components in the entire industry'.[6] Car manufacturers found it difficult enough to fit their own components together without trying to make them fit every other manufacturer's cars as well. In mechanical engineering there had been a degree of industry-wide standardization of things like screw threads and washer sizes, but assembled artefacts had never been designed to a universal module. In a

1967 *Architectural Design* article, J. F. Eden, a metrologist working at the Building Research Establishment, pointed out that, while the mechanical engineering industry had made great advances in solving interchangeability problems, it had shown no interest in 'economic size ranging' (in other words modular co-ordination) and had managed perfectly well without it. Wryly, Eden suggested that the history of modular co-ordination in building displayed 'little authentic contact with engineering' and that 'a further interchange of experience . . . might be beneficial'.[7]

Modular co-ordination, however, did not work even in its own terms. Again it was Eden who drew attention to a fundamental flaw in one of modular co-ordination's most basic tools: the reference grid. Architects had blithely postulated a regular grid – typically of 3 ft 4 in squares – to which all dimensions ultimately referred. This grid was imaginary; it existed only on drawings, though the idea for it may have originated in the stretched strings traditionally used to 'set out' a building. The practical application of this idea constantly produced accuracy problems on site. It was not uncommon for walls to be inches out of position. There may, of course, have been several reasons for this, including ordinary bad workmanship, but one reason was that, while the designers had conscientiously applied tolerance limits to their components, they had forgotten to apply them to their imaginary grid. The result was that the gaps between components were far more variable than had been assumed and the discrepancies multiplied over the length of the building. As Eden put it: 'Imaginary components can be fitted into imaginary holes, real components will fit or not fit into real holes, but fitting real components into imaginary holes . . . is metrological nonsense.' It is a fair summing up of the whole modular fallacy.

If modular co-ordination didn't work on site, it certainly didn't work in the factory. Perhaps the designers of houses, schools and hospitals really did imagine standard building components rolling off production lines in their millions. The reality was that a building programme of, say, 91 schools in 10 years did not remotely justify mass production on the Ford scale. Windows, wall panels, steel trusses, fitted cupboards – components like these were made in small batches in response to specific orders. In the building industry, mass production – the basic justification for standardization – was practically unknown.

Even standardization was largely an illusion. A study carried out by the Building Economics Research Unit uncovered a communication gap between designer and manufacturer that led architects to believe that they were standardizing to a much greater extent than they actually were.[8] The various building systems were published in the form of manuals and catalogues of available components. The versions that the architects used showed components only as basic types. An architect specifying, say, fifty 10 ft by 3 ft 4 in external wall panels for a primary school would assume that he had achieved a reasonable degree of standardization, with a consequent cost saving. However, the quantity surveyor, with access to more detailed information, would be aware that among these supposedly identical panels were many hidden variants. Finishes, for example, might vary in accordance with clauses in the written specification of which the architect was unaware. When the order reached the factory, the manufacturer would operate at yet another level of complexity. The arrangement of fixing lugs might be different for panels next to columns, panels next to doors, panels with a door on the left and a column on the right, panels with doors on both sides, and so on and on. When all the variants were combined, the number of identical panels was drastically reduced. In one example cited in the report, the architect 'saw' 229 types of component, the quantity surveyor saw 443, and the manufacturer saw 2204. So much for standardization.

The irony is that from the manufacturers' point of view, this didn't really matter very much. They were used to making components in relatively small quantities to specific orders with a high proportion of 'specials'. If it pleased the designers to imagine that they were assembling buildings from a standard kit of parts then the manufacturers were not about to disabuse them as long as the orders continued to flow. One manufacturer of pre-cast concrete panels, asked which were the standard and which the non-standard components in his product range, was unable to distinguish between them. A more serious problem from the manufacturers' point of view was the erratic nature of the ordering process. Standardization and the forming of client consortia were together supposed to consolidate demand and make it worthwhile for manufacturers to mass-produce. But if the orders all came at once because of the arrangements for the approval of finance, then what small savings standardization actually offered were far outweighed by the costs of stockpiling and double handling.

In efficiency and productivity terms, the system building approach offered few advantages and many disadvantages, not least the dull monotony of the architecture that it produced in the hands of designers less committed than the Hertfordshire pioneers. It is certain that for small and medium-size buildings, like schools, traditional construction would have performed just as well. Nevertheless system building persisted well into the 1970s and CLASP, the biggest and most famous system of them all, has even survived into the twenty-first century. According to its apologists, CLASP was and is 'the most successful, possibly the only successful British building system', but even they admit that its survival has more to do with the benefits of using 'the same team [of designers and manufacturers] in continuous collaboration'[9] than with standardization, mass production or modular co-ordination.

Just as the Hertfordshire school-building programme was reaching its modest peak of output in the early 1950s, the principles of Fordist mass-production that had inspired it were beginning to be challenged. Taiichi Ohno, a brilliant production engineer in Toyota's struggling Nagoya car factory, had visited the big American plants before the war and had returned to Japan with the intention not of copying what he saw but of completely rethinking it. Ohno and his successors were eventually to sweep aside the conventional mass-production wisdoms (the division of labour, the economies of scale, the absolute necessity for standardization) and replace them with the system, or philosophy, that is now called 'lean production'. One of the basic assumptions of mass-production had been that it was necessary to produce large numbers of identical products in order to justify investment in a dedicated production line. Once the line had been built it would remain unchanged for as long as possible to maximize production and profit. The product had to be standard-ized because any variation would necessitate a disruptive and expensive re-tooling operation. This was a principle in which practically the whole of industry believed. Ohno, however, dared to challenge it by imagining the pos-sibility of a flexible production line making a range of different products.

People were the key to Ohno's system. In Henry Ford's factories people were interchangeable components in a big machine. Assembly line workers performed the same simple tasks thousands of times a day and were told bluntly that they would be made redundant as soon as the machine to replace them had been invented. Taiichi Ohno's workers, in contrast, had jobs for life and held positions of real responsibility. They had to understand their machines and the production process as a whole because its smooth running depended on them. They were not just human robots but creative participants, carrying out the complicated adjustment and modification routines that made the flexible production line work, and making suggestions for the improvement of those routines.

But flexibility was only one aspect of Ohno's system. The main aim of lean production was to reduce waste (*muda*), not just wasted materials but wasted time and effort. Ohno saw the whole production process in terms of 'added value'. Any activity that did not add value to the product from the customer's point of view was to be minimized and, if possible, eliminated. Following the logic of this insight, Ohno began to see the production process, as it were, in reverse, from the point of view of demand rather than supply. He saw that no matter how efficient and productive a factory was, spewing out thousands of identical products at low cost was useless if the products were not what the customers wanted. Such an industry could only be successful in a world of limited choice: the world of the Model T Ford. In the modern world of increasing competition, unwanted products would pile up in warehouses (or car parks) until the price dropped to a level attractive to the customers. The cost of that warehousing was just one of the many types of *muda* that Ohno set out to eliminate. His ideal factory was one that would respond to specific demand – an actual customer's order. It would provide what the customer wanted and it would provide it immediately. Customers would, so to speak, 'pull' products out of the factory. Lean production was designed to get as close as possible to this ideal. The 'pull, don't push' principle, the obligation to fetch rather than the obligation to bring, was carried right back through the whole production process, including the outside suppliers of materials and sub-components (the 'supply chain'), so that everything from a box of screws to a completed car arrived at the next stage of the process 'just in time'.

Lean production has now replaced Fordist mass production as the ruling orthodoxy in progressive enterprises across the industrialized world. Though developed in a car factory, its principles can be applied just as readily to small-scale manufacturing, and to service industries like travel or insurance, or even medical care. In construction, or at least that sector of construction that involves architects, lean production has had little impact. Architects and architectural commentators still trot out the old arguments about the inapplicability of factory production to buildings. Here, for example, is the present author, writing in 1988:

It is economically out of the question [to emulate car production] unless identical buildings are to be produced in thousands ... The necessity for constant adaptation to different site conditions and different use requirements means that, in the end, it is usually cheaper to build in bricks and mortar.[10]

And here is Paul Barker in a *New Statesman* article about London's housing problems written in 2002:

[Prefabrication] only saves money if the units manufactured are identical, and if the factory can always run flat out. Change the specifications, or pay assembly workers for down time, while the line doesn't run at full speed, and the equations collapse.[11]

This is the old orthodoxy, out of date now that the principles of lean production are generally accepted. Flexible, responsive manufacturing on a relatively small scale suddenly seems eminently applicable to the production both of building components and of whole buildings. Standardization of the kind pursued so zealously by the system designers of the 1950s and '60s was misguided because it was based on an unrealistic view of the manufacturing part of the enterprise. The makers of steel frames and pre-cast concrete panels were not engaged in mass-production and had no need of rigid standardization. But we might look upon them (with the benefit of hindsight) as prototype lean production facilities. If the designers had been less obsessed with open systems and had paid more attention to what manufacturers actually did, then real design and production partnerships might have developed and become the norm. The subsequent retreat of prefabrication and the reassertion of the old idea that 'it is usually cheaper to build in bricks and mortar' might never have happened.

When Taiichi Ohno invented a technique that reduced the time needed to change the dies on a sheet-metal stamping machine from a whole day to just three minutes, he used only mechanical ingenuity and the skill of his workforce. But a new technology was on the way that would soon join forces with lean production to break the mass production spell and open up a new world of variety and choice. In 1952 the first numerically controlled machine tool was made for the US Air Force in a research laboratory at MIT. It was the start of an infiltration of digital technology into manufacturing that would culminate in the concept of Computer Integrated Manufacturing (CIM), in other words a whole factory controlled by a computer. The acronyms proliferate: AMT (Advanced Manufacturing Technologies), FMS (Flexible Manufacturing Systems), CNC (Computer Numerical Control), MV (Machine Vision), AMH (Automatic Materials Handling), AGV (Automated Guided Vehicles, used instead of old-fashioned conveyor belts), AS/RS (Automatic Storage and Retrieval), CPM (Computerised Process Monitoring) and, of course, JIT (Just In Time). Together perhaps they conjure up at least a vague picture of the modern automated factory.

But the important one from a designer's point of view is CAM (Computer Aided Manufacturing). It is important because it dispenses once and for all with the necessity for standardization. A computer-controlled machine can make a hundred different components in almost the same time that it takes to make a hundred identical ones. For example, a thermal cutting machine can accurately and continuously cut out a hundred shapes, all different, from a sheet of aluminium, following a CAD (Computer Aided Design) drawing like a dressmaker's pattern. (The CAD program automatically works out the most economical arrangement of the shapes on the sheet.) The architectural practice called Future Systems used this technique, borrowed from the boat-building

The roof of the British Museum's Great Court, by Norman Foster.

industry, to form the blob-shaped Media Centre at Lord's Cricket Ground. A router can make mortice and tenon joints of different sizes in different positions on a hundred different pieces of wood without pausing for adjustment. The variations in the standard panels of a 1960s system-built school would these days therefore present no problem. A multi-axis lathe can make a hundred spherical steel space-frame nodes with the threaded holes all at different angles. The rods that connect the nodes can all be different too, in length and thickness. It is this technology that makes possible the irregular, structurally organic shapes of space frames like the roof of the Great Court at the British Museum, designed by Norman Foster.

The freedom of form and dimension that CAM allows, allied to the flexibility of lean production, makes the non-standard factory-made building a real possibility. The customer – a house buyer, for example – really could have whatever he or she wanted, just like the single client of a traditional architect but without the fees and the risk. The limitations would be human, not technical. Consumers are not designers or inventors and products would still have to be developed and tested, especially if they departed from traditional forms. In practice the choice would have to be either a variation on one of a range of semi-standard models, or a combination of semi-standard components. In other words the products would be both mass-produced and custom-made.

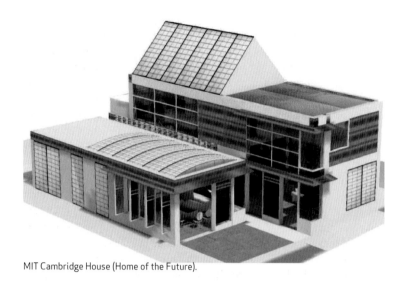
MIT Cambridge House (Home of the Future).

'Mass Customization' is what the rest of industry calls it. Car manufacturers now look upon their products as a range of components – chassis, bodies, engines, wiring harnesses, seats, interior linings, dashboards, radios etc. – that can be put together in different combinations. Sometimes the possible combinations are hidden from the customer (a Citroën fitted with another body becomes a Peugeot) and sometimes they are made explicit so that customers can choose the features they want. Of course there is nothing new about car buyers having a choice, say of colour or trim, but in the past, under the old mass production system, manufacturers had to predict the level of demand for each feature and stockpile as necessary, hoping they had predicted right. Under the lean production system, assisted by computer-controlled machinery, cars can be 'built to order' (BTO), which enormously increases the number of possible component combinations.

Kent Larson, an architect and researcher in MIT's Home of the Future laboratory, wants to apply mass customization to housing. He envisages a near future in which companies as different as IKEA and BMW will manufacture house components. They will supply them to 'integrators' hosting websites on which customers use friendly CAD software to design their own homes, combining components from one or more ranges and perhaps, while they are there, signing up for services such as mortgages and medical insurance. 'Ordering their home', says Larson, '[will be] no more complicated than buying an automobile on-line.'[12] Larson's vision is seductive and provocative, although he falls into the trap of assuming that anything new must necessarily be electronic. The components will, he says, include 'sensor arrays and digital displays' so that the house can automatically adjust itself to the occupant's lifestyle, setting the right light levels and keeping the refrigerator stocked. He may be right, but in the broader view of the transformation of house building these are just gimmicks. On the other hand, Larson fails to note that the essential functions of the integrator's website are already performed by consumer CAD software and well-established Web versions of the old-fashioned pattern book (see Chapter 5). He also wants manufacturers to agree 'open architectural standards', based on the international standards used in the computer industry, 'to foster desperately needed innovation in the housing industry'. This sounds suspiciously like the old open system mentality – a brake on innovation, not a spur to it. And Larson's is a characteristically American vision of ideal housing in which the individual detached house is the norm. Applying it in Europe, where collective forms are the norm, may be more problematic.

Nevertheless mass customization is a useful concept to apply to the production of everyday buildings like houses and schools. Lean production and computer-aided manufacturing have abolished all the old mass production imperatives, including modular co-ordination and the use of regulating grids. Dimensions and proportions no longer need to be standardized in order to facilitate efficient production. We might reflect, however, remembering Brunelleschi, that that was not the reason they were standardized in the first place.

# 7. Ideal homes

Foamboard is a 5-mm thick sandwich of coated paper and expanded poly-styrene, useful for mounting posters or making simple three-dimensional objects such as point-of-sale displays. It can also be used to make architectural models, though it is often frowned upon by teachers in architecture schools because of its unsympathetic visual and tactile qualities. Natural materials like balsa wood or plain grey card tend to be preferred. Foamboard models are also said to encourage a tendency among students to ignore the structural and constructional aspects of their designs (beams and columns, the depths of floors, the thicknesses of walls) and deal only with abstracted form and space. Real buildings, so the argument goes, are not made from universal structural boards of even thickness, cut to shape and glued together. Well, this view may have to change, because in the US houses are increasingly being made in exactly that way. The universal boards are called SIPS (Structural Insulated Panels) and buildings made from them are just like full-size versions of foamboard models. Panels are usually about 150 mm thick, with a rigid insulating foam core sandwiched between two continuously bonded sheets of plywood or, more commonly, oriented strand board (OSB). And that's all. A SIPS wall works on the stressed-skin principle. It is capable of supporting upper floors and roofs in much the same way as a brick wall or a wooden frame. And the panels really are glued together, at the corners and edge to edge. They are light and easy to handle and they make virtually airtight enclosures with very high thermal insulation values. They also lend them-selves well to prefabrication and customization. House kits can be made up in the factory from panels cut out on numerically controlled or CAD/CAM machines. SIPS houses are usually clad with a rainscreen of boards or tiles, but in theory the OSB could simply be painted.

The SIPS method currently accounts for about 6 per cent of US house build-ing and is growing rapidly. In one sense SIPS is a new technology, but in another it is only the latest branch of the big family of lightweight construction methods

SIPS panel joint.

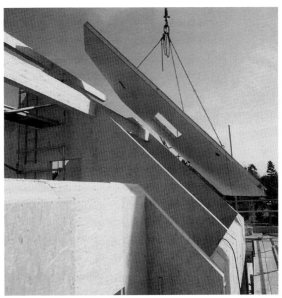

House under construction using the Tekhaus SIPS system.

descended from the old balloon frame. Over the 170 years since its invention the balloon frame has proved remarkably adaptable. The most basic adaptation is the platform frame, in which the floors are constructed as distinct structural units or platforms, and the walls are framed as storey-height panels. The platform frame has now largely superseded the balloon frame. It is more manageable and more flexible, lending itself to a variety of different building methods. It can be 'stick-built' on site in the traditional way; it can be 'panel-built', the wall and floor panels being framed up in a factory and delivered to the site on a lorry; or it can be 'box-built', the panels being made up into room-size

Platform frame house under construction.

'modules' in the factory. But the differences between the three methods are largely illusory. All platform frame houses are made from sticks, panels and boxes, in that order. It is simply a question of where each phase of the construction takes place. From the point of view of quality, it is best to do as much as possible in the factory for a hundred reasons: more space, better access and visibility, better working conditions, more equipment, closer supervision and so on.

The balloon frame buildings of the Wild West were mostly shacks and barns, basic shells with no trimmings. Modern houses have to be insulated, lined, heated, cooled, wired and plumbed-in. Should these extras be fitted on site or in the factory? From the design point of view it hardly matters. This is the beauty of the balloon frame and its derivatives. They lend themselves readily to any degree of prefabrication. Some factories make only frames, leaving everything else to be fitted on site. Others make finished wall panels, or 'cassettes', complete with siding, insulation quilt, vapour barrier, drywall lining, door and window frames, glass and wiring. They might even be painted. And the box makers do even more in the factory. Hotel and motel chains often use 'modular' systems in which each hotel room is a separate box that arrives on the site locked shut. On opening day it is unlocked to reveal a finished interior with everything in place, including the pictures on the wall (see Chapter 8).

A change of structural material, from timber studs to light-gauge steel studs for example, doesn't make a construction system any less a balloon frame derivative. The same stick/panel/box options apply and the finished building will probably be outwardly indistinguishable from its wooden relative. Even more radical innovations, such as in monocoque or semi-monocoque structures using polymer composite or stressed skin panels, including SIPS, are often developments of balloon or platform frame prototypes. A SIPS house is simply a balloon frame house without the frame.

But not all prefabricated houses are descended from the balloon frame house. Border Oak is a small Herefordshire firm producing about 60 bespoke houses a year for the upper sector of the self-build market. It is one of the very few British house builders experienced in the latest SIPS technology. Its speciality, however, is traditional English timber-framed houses: not fake half-timbered houses, but real post-and-beam structures of green oak infilled with the modern equivalent of wattle and daub. (All oak-framed buildings use 'green' oak; seasoned oak is very scarce and would be too hard to work.) The two technologies are represented by two buildings on the company's factory site. At the front of the site, facing the road, is a two-storey, oak-framed building that doubles as front office and show house. Behind it sits a somewhat larger office

SIPS building at Border Oak's Herefordshire headquarters.

extension that looks like a converted barn with its plain tiled roof and clap-boarded walls, but is actually made from SIPS. Sometimes Border Oak combines the two technologies in a single building. One of its pattern book house designs shows an oak inner structure, or 'aisle frame', enveloped in a SIPS external wall: the most traditional and ruggedly expressive structural material combined with the most modern and cardboard-like.

Border Oak's cavalier attitude to history and technology is problematic for those brought up to believe in certain architectural principles. Modernist dogma insists, first, that a building should be of its time and not pretend to be older than it is and, second, that technologies should be honestly expressed and not imitate other technologies. These two principles are linked. 'Of its time' implies the use of up-to-date technology. Now if Border Oak were simply faking its half-timbering, like a hundred other house builders, it could immediately be convicted on both counts and dismissed as a vulgar commercial operation of no cultural worth. (This would not necessarily be fair or logical but it would be the normal architectural response.) But Border Oak's half-timbering is real, using traditional dowelled mortice and tenon joints. So it fails on the first count but passes on the second, setting up an uncomfortable ideological feedback loop. Nobody would mind if this were a building restoration business (which in fact was how it started). Perfectly respectable architectural reputations have been built on the sensitive restoration and adaptation of old oak-framed buildings. But Border Oak's houses are all new, machine-made in a factory and marketed by the American pattern book method. Two local draughtsmen, father and son, produce dozens of 'standard' designs, with names like Forgetmenot Cottage, Honeysuckle Farmhouse and Barleymow Manor, drawn in an appealing freehand style for publication in brochures and on the Internet. But these are really just suggestions to help clients decide what they want. In the end, all houses are bespoke. When the design of an actual house is finalized, one of the draughtsmen will prepare a seductive set of drawings for the local planners. Then, after the contract is signed, a different, CAD draughtsman will produce the shop drawings for the cutting of the oak. The frame is completely prefabricated, leaving the factory as a bundle of coded posts and beams that have already been trial-assembled. This is not so different from the way it was done 400 years ago.

Another Border Oak paradox is that the boss of the company, John Greene, turns out to be an architect who qualified by part-time study after founding the business. This might account for the high degree of literacy of the designs. A Border Oak house is a pastiche, but a knowing one that draws on considerable historical knowledge. John Greene's daughter, Mary Albright, who works for the company, has an MSc in vernacular building, for which she studied

Border Oak pattern book perspective.

Trial assembly of an oak frame in Border Oak's factory.

Precut frame of a large house ready for delivery.

under oak-frame expert Richard Harris. Information packs given to potential customers include a copy of Harris's book, *Discovering Timber Framed Buildings*. Customers are expected to care about the historical aspects of their purchases, whether, for example, they want a close-studded frame of the Sussex type or a square-panelled frame typical of the Midlands and the Welsh Borders. So a Border Oak house is designed by an architect in a pre-architectural style, using a structural form usually regarded as obsolete but prefabricated in a modern factory from a combination natural oak and the latest synthetic, industrially produced materials. A vernacular building tradition, once the only way to build, is now sold as one of a number of technical and stylistic choices in an expanding market. In a sense it's a fake, but people buy it because it's genuine. Paradoxical indeed.

'Self-build' is a misleading phrase, not to be taken literally. It means simply buying a plot of land and arranging for a house to be built on it for owner occupation. The owner may or may not participate in the actual building process. In the US, Scandinavia and Japan, self-build is normal; in Britain, where speculative house building is the norm, self-build is regarded as an adventurous and risky lifestyle choice. But it is growing. Thirty years ago it was mostly limited to the very rich, who employed architects, or the relatively poor, who built with their own hands, sometimes using the Segal method, a simplified softwood post-and-beam system designed specifically for amateur builders by the modernist architect Walter Segal. Now, 25 per cent of detached houses are self-built, most of them by families who, though not rich, are well enough off to afford four bedrooms, an en-suite bathroom and a double garage. Self-build has become an industry with its own identity, promoted in specialist magazines, trade exhibitions and television programmes.

Several types of design and construction service have evolved to meet the demand. The Association of Self-build Architects (ASBA), founded in 1992, is an alliance of small practices (maximum six professional staff each) who market themselves as the modest and approachable wing of the profession. But, for the most part, self-builders steer clear of professional architects who have a reputation in the industry for designing what they think the client should have rather than what the client actually wants. Most self-builders are not interested in becoming architectural patrons and are happier with the straightforward buyer-seller relationship offered by package deal companies. A package dealer will design and manage a project, including getting planning permission and building regulation approval, on the understanding that the customer buys the bulk of materials and components from the company. It may be left to the customer to find their own builder, or the company may offer a complete 'design and build' service.

Technically speaking, specialist systems like green oak and SIPS account for only a tiny proportion of the self-build market, which is mainly divided into two camps: load-bearing brick and block versus prefabricated timber frame. Traditionalists favour brick and block. In Britain, 'bricks and mortar' are regarded as a safe investment, while the 170-year-old technology of the timber frame is seen as dangerously experimental. It may be true that timber is more vulnerable in Britain's damp climate, but the public's willingness to believe scare stories is probably a bigger factor. In May 1983 the then growing timber-frame housing industry was stopped in its tracks by a 'World in Action' television programme about technical failures. Improved detailing, in particular the use of 'breather membranes' to prevent hidden condensation, has led to a partial rehabilitation of timber frame's reputation. But in a country where the monetary value of a house is often more important than its functional value, the suspicion persists that a timber-frame house will put off some buyers and therefore depress the price. A partial solution, and one that is adopted almost universally, is to hide the timber frame behind a non-load-bearing skin of brickwork. Technically, this is likely to do more harm than good. Indeed the whole concept of the double-leaf, cavity wall, a peculiarly British form of construction, is arguably becoming obsolete as building regulations require higher and higher insulation values. But the market demands brick walls and the private housing industry will continue to supply them. Recently, several brick substitute products have come onto the market. There are two types. The first is a prefabricated panel faced with thin brick 'slips', glued on and pointed with mortar. The second is a version of tile hanging. Clay tiles are specially shaped so that when hung on a timber-framed wall they create a flush surface similar to brickwork. This is not a new idea. In the late eighteenth century it was called 'mathematical tiling' and was applied to many timber-framed town houses in the south-east of England in an attempt to enhance their architectural status.

This whole brickwork question is interesting because it locates very precisely the dividing line between architectural and non-architectural taste. Architects generally disapprove of the use of brickwork as a non-load-bearing cladding. The work of Michael Hopkins is an extreme case in point. Brought up in the strict High Tech church and therefore coming to brickwork relatively late in his career, Hopkins vowed to use it only as a 'real' structural material. In large buildings like Glyndebourne Opera House and the Inland Revenue building in Nottingham he used load-bearing brickwork where any other architect would have used a steel or concrete frame and, if necessary, clad it in non-load-bearing brickwork. Curiously, in the Nottingham building the brickwork piers were actually prefabricated to save time on site, but they were made of real bricks and they bore real loads, so the vow was honoured. Not all architects are as dogmatic as Hopkins and many would happily tolerate non-load-bearing brick skins. Glued-on brick slips, however, are shunned implacably by all architects. Architectural approval of the mathematical tiling type of pseudo-brickwork will depend on how it is detailed. Whereas builders usually arrange the tiles in stretcher bond, with staggered vertical joints, because it looks like brickwork, architects tend to prefer stack bond, with continuous vertical joints, because it doesn't look like brickwork and is therefore not dishonest. The cladding of the famous Murray Grove modular housing scheme (see Chapter 8) is a good example.

The big advantage of timber frame over load-bearing brick is that it lends itself to prefabrication, which shortens the on-site build time. Whereas in the US 'stick building' is still common, in Britain and the rest of Europe timber-frame houses are almost always prefabricated to some extent. Prefabricated does not mean mass produced, or even standardized. British companies like Potton, Custom Homes and Kingpost Design publish pattern books that seem to offer standard designs, but in practice every house for the self-build market is made to order and a high degree of customization is normal. The main structural components of the house – walls, floors and roof trusses – might all arrive on site on the same day. It is tempting, therefore, to refer to them as a 'kit'. There is something about that word 'kit' that appeals to everybody – architects, builders and house buyers alike. It seems to promise every building virtue: speed, economy, quality, reliability. An image is called to mind of the arrival on site of a nest of boxes, small containers perhaps, from which emerge pre-finished panels ready to be hoisted into position and bolted together with some kind of heavy-duty Allen key, like outsize self-assembly furniture. People have even started to talk about 'flat-pack' houses. The reality is less appealing. Building projects almost always turn out to be more complicated than was first envisaged, even by hardened professionals. There are foundations to be dug, site irregularities to be accommodated, ill-fitting components to be modified on site, and dozens of carcassing and second fix operations that must be carried out laboriously by hand. Putting up a basic, weatherproof enclosure in as short a time as possible is a good strategy to adopt, but there is still a long way to go after that.

Still, there was great excitement when it was announced in 1996 that the Swedish furniture company IKEA, undisputed masters of self-assembly, flat-pack technology, had started producing houses. This, surely, would be the realization of the kit house dream. The house was given a funny Swedish name, BoKlok (roughly 'live smart'), just like the Billy bookcases, Pax wardrobes and Attityd kitchen units familiar to IKEA addicts everywhere, and before long it was being vigorously marketed throughout Scandinavia and in

IKEA Bo Klok flats.

Britain. Disappointingly, however, BoKlok turned out to be not an individual house for the self-build market, but a small block of flats to be built speculatively. It also looked rather ordinary, though likeable enough: a two-storey, communal version of a traditional Swedish summer house. The one-, two- and three-bedroom flats were cleverly planned, with no corridors, and the whole package was made more attractive to its relatively low-income target market by an allocation of free furniture vouchers. But it would never have attracted the attention of the colour supplements had it not borne the IKEA brand name. The phrase 'IKEA house' had conjured up that appealing kit house image in everyone's mind, but in truth BoKlok was nothing to do with either self-build or flat-pack. Developed in partnership with contracting giant Skanska and timber frame manufacturer Myresjöhus, it actually did not deviate far from standard Swedish house building practice.

In Sweden there is no timber frame versus brickwork debate, no awkward compromises, no ideological agonizing. The balloon or platform frame has been the standard technology for low-rise housing ever since it took over from the log building vernacular in the early twentieth century. Self-build is common too, growing out of a long tradition of building summer houses. In the 1920s the City of Stockholm provided standard house plans and pre-cut timber to encourage working class families to build their own houses in the suburbs. In the 1950s and '60s, sawmills began to diversify into the production of house components, such as roof trusses and wall panels, taking advantage of timber frame's natural aptitude for prefabrication. Soon the industry had settled into a tripartite structure: the factory itself; a marketing operation producing advertisements and brochures, including pattern books; and a network of builders to assemble the individual houses on site. Dozens of small companies now operate in this way. It has become the normal method of housing provision in a country where almost half of households live in privately owned detached houses.

Swedish house manufacturers collaborate with one another to the extent of building show houses on shared permanent exhibition sites. The HusExpo at Skondal on the outskirts of Gothenburg, for example, displays more than 60 houses, representing about 30 manufacturers, only slightly more densely laid out than they would be in a typical Swedish suburb. Walking among these houses, what strikes an English visitor is their relatively uncorrupted vernacular style. There are occasional eruptions of 'architecture' – a triangular window or a showy balcony – but for the most part the national building tradition holds sway and the result is a pleasing consistency, not only of construction but of colour, texture, proportion and detail. These industrially produced and mass-marketed houses are still just recognizable as the descendants of early twentieth-century workers' houses, such as those in the Landala residential quarter of Gothenburg. Laid out in the garden city manner on a rocky, sloping site between 1908 and 1922, Landala was a product of the Home-Owners movement, a government initiative providing workers with cheap housing loans to dissuade them from emigrating. The estate still exists, its gardens wonderfully mature, its houses obviously much loved, their red pantile roofs and wooden walls weathered to perfection. Indeed they might almost be part of a BoKlok development such as the one in Malmö, which is treated in sober brown stain rather than the more cheerful, though equally traditional, red, yellow or blue.

Swedish private house builders, who mostly build in wood, are almost all factory-based. Their British counterparts, the speculative 'volume builders', who mostly build in brick, are almost all site-based. Some would argue that they are site-based to an extreme, unhealthy degree. Operating as management contractors, they hold very few fixed assets, apart from land banks, and

A street in the HusExpo
at Skondal.

HusExpo house:
traditional with
occasional eruptions
of 'architecture'.

Landala suburb, Gothenburg.

they employ almost nobody directly, relying instead on labour sub-contractors, often self-employed individuals. It sounds like a recipe for inefficiency and poor quality, and it is, but it wasn't laziness or stupidity that gave rise to it. As a recent government-sponsored report points out, it makes perfect sense in its economic context:

> It follows from decades of free market response to a demand that fluctuates quite widely from location to location and year to year, and is focused obsessively on first cost (rather than running costs, quality, reliability or any of those other classic manufacturing mantras). The result is a highly elastic, extremely low cost delivery system that makes no demands on risk capital. Indeed some of the better-organised medium-size builders come close to being the ideal 'virtual company'.[1]

The product of this system is what architects contemptuously call 'Noddy houses' – little pitched-roofed, two-storey brick boxes clustering round cul-de-sacs on the outskirts of every English town. Fashions in speculative housing change every decade or so. There was a time in the 1950s and '60s when rational cross-wall construction and communal landscaping almost made it architecturally respectable. One well-known architect, Eric Lyons, went so far to found his own development company, Span, which built well-planned,

The Ideal Home Exhibition House of the Future, 1928.

picturesque modern estates for the discerning middle classes in London's southern suburbs. But mostly volume house building has been a no-go area for architects. Their arms-length relationship with it is perhaps best illustrated by the Daily Mail Ideal Home Exhibition, held almost every year in London since 1908. The exhibition always includes several full-size show houses, constructed inside one of the big exhibition halls at either Earls Court or Olympia, and usually one of them is designed by a real, named architect. In recent years the special architect-designed house has been called a 'concept house' (like the concept cars at the Motor Show) and has been selected on the basis of a design competition. In 2000 the winner was the 'Hanger House', designed by Michael Kohn and Katy Ghahremani, an exercise in customization by means of an interactive computer program; the previous year it was the Slim House, by Pierre d'Avoine, a reinterpretation of the traditional terraced house for mass production; and the year before that it was the 'Oyster House', by Nigel Coates, a fun flying saucer on legs.

But the concept house is just the latest incarnation of the old House of the Future. The very first Ideal Home House of the Future appeared in the 1928 exhibition and was designed by the architects S. Rowland Pierce and R. A. Duncan. A flat-roofed, modernist box, it had a stainless-steel frame clad in an imaginary plastic material (not yet invented), wind-down car windows, roller shutter partitions, electric underfloor heating and a garage for an triphibious 'aerocar'. The *Daily Mail* article, subtitled 'An Architect's Daring Prophecy' concluded:

It is a house not built to last for centuries, but only until such time as progress makes it or any of its parts out of date. Then renewal, it is said, is merely a matter of ordering a new model or a new part – just as you would in the case of a motor car![2]

But if architects occupy a special position in the Ideal Home Exhibition, it is never the central position. They are allowed to design the houses of the future, but not the houses of the present. Their creations are usually off to one side, leaving the axial view clear for this year's star attraction, likely to be a clumsy confection of fake half-timbering or cartoon classicism. This is symbolic of the real position of architects in relation to the house-building industry. In the shrivelled public sector, which is not much more than 10 per cent of total housing output, clients tend to play safe and employ an independent architect, but private house builders mostly manage without, relying on in-house technicians and draughtsmen. Noddy houses, with their vaguely cottage-like forms and their stuck-on vernacular details, may represent the lowest level of design imagination, but they are very cheap to build and they sell well enough just as they are.

Technically, most volume-built housing is 'traditional', with load-bearing brick and block walls, wooden floors and sloping, tile-covered roofs. But that word 'traditional' has to be qualified. It doesn't mean crafted on site using centuries-old materials and techniques. How traditional can a building be that incorporates polyurethane insulation, pressure-impregnated timber, chipboard flooring, pressed steel lintels, plastic window frames and a dozen other materials unknown 50 years ago? Recent additions to the repertoire of commonly used factory-made components include pre-cast concrete floor planks (for better sound insulation and quicker ground floor construction), open lattice floor joists (easier to pass wires and pipes through) and structural insulated roof panels (offering straightforward later conversion of loft spaces). The parts that make up the average Noddy house are technically rather advanced. It is the often shoddy way they are put together that infuriates house buyers and worries the government's industry watchers.

The realization has dawned that in the last 20 years, since Margaret Thatcher's 'right to buy' policy effectively put an end to publicly financed and built 'council housing', Britain has not been building enough houses. There is a lot of catching up to do. Planning restrictions are being relaxed and the talk is all of 'sustainable communities'. But can the volume builders, with their low levels of investment, their site-based technologies and their ad hoc supply chains, really be entrusted with a programme to produce 4.4 million new homes by 2016? The general opinion is no, not without some fundamental reforms. The government thinks that house builders should invest in factory production and begin making reliable, high-quality houses that are cheap to run as well as cheap to build. It is beginning to encourage prefabrication, just as it did in the 1960s. For example, a £300 million Housing Corporation programme to build 6,000 new homes for key workers in London and the Southeast in 2003–4 insisted that at least 1,800 of them should be built 'using modern, off-site construction techniques'.[3]

Increasing demand is not the only pressure pushing builders towards prefabrication. Thirty years of decline have eaten away at the industry's skill base. The average age of a bricklayer in the UK is climbing into the upper fifties and there are no big training initiatives on the horizon. 'Virtual companies' who rely on sub-contract labour are not well placed to nurture apprentices. And no doubt the gradual increase in the number of factory-made building components has played its part in undermining traditional craft skills. Installing a plastic window requires little in the way of specialist joinery skills (though it is essential to be able to follow the instructions on the packet). Of course factory workers also need to be trained, but as the history of the American mobile home industry shows, factory training is a lot faster and cheaper.

Some British house builders are responding to these pressures and experimenting with factory-based systems. The technology is the usual repertoire of variations on the balloon frame: panels and/or modules made from either wood or light steel, plus the occasional foray into SIPS or pre-cast concrete. One of the biggest and best-equipped operations is Space4, set up by house builders Westbury with help from Warwick University's Manufacturing Group. The 22,000-square-metre factory near Birmingham makes timber-framed closed panels filled with injected phenolic insulating foam that forms a bond with the inner and outer boards. It is therefore a hybrid of timber-frame and SIPS technology. Wall panels have built-in conduits for heating, plumbing and electrics, and doors and windows are fitted in the factory. Floors are also prefabricated in the form of 'cassettes' using wooden I-beams instead of softwood joists. None of this is very unusual. What makes the Space4 factory different is the level of investment in automation. The production line is a moving track and the CAD/CAM-operated machines are capable of making customized panels, all different, without pausing to rejig. The total capacity of the factory is reckoned to be about 5,500 houses a year, which makes it almost comparable with some of the big Japanese manufacturers (see Chapter 9).

Steel construction for housing is vigorously promoted by the Steel Construction Institute, which publishes excellent technical literature covering all aspects of the use of cold formed steel (CFS), from stick building, through

Space4 factory.

panels to full-blown modular. The Surebuild system, now into its third phase
of development, is manufactured and marketed by Framing Solutions, a joint
venture between Corus (which used to be British Steel) and the house builder
Redrow. The company supplies several house builders with customized wall
panels and floor cassettes made in its CAD/CAM-equipped factory in
Derbyshire.

In the architectural way of thinking, all this new technology ought to be
transforming British house design. But it isn't. The average CFS or SIPS house
is indistinguishable from its site-built cousins. The brick cladding habit has yet
to be broken and in any case house builders do not think architecturally. There
are one or two exceptions. Sunley Homes, for example, imported 'Super E'
timber frames from Canada for its Lacuna development at West Malling in
Kent and asked Canterbury architects Clague to design the houses. Super E is
the brand name not of a single system, but of a Canadian government standard, originally designed to promote exports to Japan. The timber frame itself
is fairly conventional except that the external walls are completely airtight,

Lacuna develop-
ment at Kings Hill,
West Malling.

which improves insulation and saves energy. Windows can be opened, but when they are closed a simple mechanical ventilation system, with heat recovery, maintains a healthy internal environment. Features like this benefit the occupant directly rather than just making life easier for the builder. They therefore demand to be marketed, and one way to do that is to make the houses look different. Clague have designed an informal arrangement of two- and three-storey houses, mostly clad in white imitation wood clapboarding, which looks fresher and sharper than the average cul de sac. Interiors are well lit and spatially complex, with double-height rooms, galleries, glazed stairwells and bigger than normal windows.

Lacuna is part of a larger development called Kings Hill on the site of an old RAF airfield. Several developers have contributed to it over the years, creating a mosaic of stylistic enclaves. There is plenty of neo-Georgian of varying degrees of literacy, the usual allowance of fake half-timbering and some vaguely American-looking streets, with houses in approximately Dutch Colonial or New England styles. A popular new style, though a style of site layout rather

'Neo Poundbury' develop-
ment at Kings Hill.

than of detail, is what might be called neo-Poundbury, after the development
sponsored by the Prince of Wales on the outskirts of Dorchester in Dorset.
Instead of being strung out along streets, houses are tightly clustered around
mews courts, their fronts facing outwards onto narrow brick-paved roads with
no front gardens. House types are jumbled together, three-storey next to two-
storey, stuccoed symmetry next to rustic Kentish tile-hanging, as if they were
built in different centuries.

Kings Hill and other similar upmarket developments (Ingress Park in
Greenhithe and St Mary's Island in Chatham are two more examples in Kent)
are reminiscent of American New Urbanist developments like Celebration,
Seaside and their imitators (see Chapter 5). The marketing suites and interior
designed show houses are almost as lavish, and house buyers must feel that they
are buying a self-image as much as a place to live. Still this is a partial version,
lacking the up-front clarity of the American originals. There are no security
gates, no age restrictions, no exclusive leisure facilities, no Art of Living
Directors to encourage social activities among the residents. Indeed it is unclear
quite why it should be thought necessary to style and theme a British housing
estate in this way. Do customers insist on it? Is it the result of pressure from

planners to imitate to the local vernacular? Or is it simply that developers have been seduced by their own sumptuous brochures? This is a discussion to which architects might well make a useful contribution, provided they are willing to be sensitive to popular taste.

One thing is clear. The appearance of private housing estates has nothing to do with the way they are built. For many architects, this is precisely what is wrong with them. It isn't that the wrong styles are chosen, or that the styles are misunderstood and mishandled. The problem is with the whole concept of style. Why, architects say, can't a house just be a straightforward expression of its construction? If it is site-built in brick then let it be brick and don't dress it up with half-timbering. If the structure is a timber frame, then board it or tile-hang it but don't build a brick wall round it. But this is a misguided view. House buyers know nothing about construction and don't care about its honest expression. More interestingly, builders don't care about it either. It is an idea exclusive to architecture, and it isn't even a particularly clever idea. To forbid the construction of fake façades or the translation of form from one material to another would wipe out most of the historical canon that gives modern architecture its legitimacy, including the whole of the classical tradition. Far better to accept, as house builders do, that construction and style are separate, that a brick wall does not necessarily bear any load, and that timber boarding may well be covering up load-bearing blockwork. It is not possible to abolish style. 'Architect designed' is a style. 'Prefabricated' could conceivably become a style, and it wouldn't necessarily be applied to prefabricated buildings.

There are signs that the house-buying public is becoming more aware of style and getting harder to please. When the fashion designer Wayne Hemingway complained in the press about the 'Wimpification of Britain', house builders Wimpey asked him to contribute design ideas to an affordable housing development in Gateshead. The Gateshead scheme is unremarkable, incorporating features such as communal gardens and traffic segregation that were common in architect-designed public housing schemes 30 years ago. But two things are interesting about the Hemingway episode: first, that even in a seller's market Wimpey felt the need to improve its image, and second, that to do so it called in a fashion designer, not an architect.

There is a feeling that the old stylistic formulae are getting tired and that the public would welcome something new, but nobody is quite sure what. The growing self-build market might provide a clue, particularly the commonest type of self-build, house extensions, and more particularly the commonest type of house extension, the conservatory. Research carried out by Ultraframe, Britain's biggest conservatory manufacturer, reveals that there are 11.6 million houses in the UK that could feasibly be extended by the addition of a conserva-

Victorian-style
conservatory by
Moore windows.

tory. Two million houses already have conservatories and of the remainder about 5.6 million are owned by the sort of people who just might be persuaded that a conservatory is what they need. Conservatories are currently being manufactured at the rate of 200,000 per year and output is increasing rapidly. At the current rate of growth, in ten years or so the market will be saturated and Britain will have become Conservatory Land. But by then the earliest factory-made conservatories built back in the 1980s will need replacing and new markets in Europe and the US will be opening up.

The phenomenal success of the conservatory tells us a lot about people's relationships with their homes. It also hints at a different way to provide homes. Consider the qualities of the conservatory. It is a luxury item, built for the sheer enjoyment of space and light. Factory-made from synthetic materials, it is a standard product that can be inspected in advance in showrooms and brochures, but is offered in a choice of sizes, prices, styles and colours. (Victorian is by far the most popular style, but it is mostly a matter of plastic stick-on cornices and finials. Conservatories without Victorian details are called Mediterranean.) Perhaps the most important quality of the conservatory is precisely that it is not a house, only a specialized part of a house. This suggests that a whole house might be conceived as a collection of specialized parts – bathrooms, kitchens, bedrooms, hallways, studies, carports, garden sheds – manufactured and marketed like conservatories. Ultraframe's factory in Clitheroe, Lancashire, is a perfect example of mass customization in action. Hundreds of conservatory kits are assembled there every day from aluminium and PVC extrusions cut on numerically controlled machines. And every kit has an individual customer's name on it.

# 8. Little boxes

The box is a useful invention for putting things in and carrying things around. Boxes, plural, are even more useful, especially if they are the same size and stackable. They tidy up the world's property, organizing it and keeping track of it. Matchboxes, shoe boxes, wine crates, tea chests – at about this point on the scale special handling tools become necessary: stepladders, trolleys, fork-lift trucks, travelling cranes. And the question arises: what is the optimum size for a box? The answer, we now know, is twenty feet long by eight feet wide by eight feet high. It's called an ISO (International Standards Organisation) shipping container. Some containers are 40 feet long, but the volume of international freight, other than bulk commodities like oil or gravel, is these days almost universally measured in TEUs, or Twenty foot Equivalent Units.

The container is simply a stackable steel box sized to suit the transport networks of the world. It was not until the 1950s that Malcolm McClean, an American trucking entrepreneur, persuaded port authorities and freight carriers to stop gazing into the cavernous holds of ships and turn their attention instead to the long, narrow forms of the lorries, trains and barges that carried the goods to and from the port. McClean started by simply lashing the trailers of his trucks to the decks of ships instead of unloading small boxes one at a time from truck to hold. There were lots of advantages to the new method. It was faster, more secure and required much less labour. But to get the most out of it, to achieve real transport 'intermodality', investment was required in new handling equipment and bigger ships. In 1956 the first true container ship, the *Ideal X*, sailed from Newark, New Jersey, and the tooling-up of Port Elizabeth, the first true container port, began. Now freight liners have themselves become mere floating boxes, enormous container containers, and every major seaport in the world is fitted with the necessary gantries, saddle-carriers and quay-cranes to lift and shift containers. Huge multistorey container mega-structures, absolutely regular and temptingly architectural, are continuously constructed and deconstructed like modular cities of the future.

Container port, Barcelona.

Container site hut.

Containers have not changed much in essence in fifty years, although there are now different kinds for different cargoes: side-opening, end-opening, open-topped, collapsible, 'flatracks', 'hangertainers', and air conditioned 'reefers'. The idea that a shipping container might be used not as a box but as a building, that it might even be inhabited, was obvious right from the start. If you need a secure store for materials on a building site, for example, a big box made of sheet steel that arrives ready-made on a lorry is ideal. And you only need to hack a couple of holes in the side for windows, and perhaps fit a human-size door instead of the big end-flaps, to make a very serviceable site office. Containers used completely unselfconsciously as temporary accommodation are commonplace. In the Royal Air Force Museum at Hendon there is even a container fitted out as an airfield chapel, complete with miniature campanile.

But can containers be architecture? For the right clients on the right site, perhaps they can. The architect Nicolas Lacey used converted containers to make a cluster of small artists' studios in London's Docklands area, near the old lighthouse at Trinity Buoy Wharf. But the design uses containers for their photogenic rather than their technical or functional qualities, and by welding the containers together, it completely ignores their essentially portable nature. Penoyre and Prasad's temporary children's nursery in Bloomsbury for the Treehouse Trust is more convincing. Here a cladding of narrow horizontal larch battens makes ordinary steel containers with square windows look like slick minimalist modules. The two-storey building has been 'parked' between mature plane trees causing little disruption and looking perfectly inoffensive.

These architectural flirtations with the container industry are unlikely to blossom into large-scale commercial production. Container suppliers themselves, however, long ago realized the potential of their products as buildings and have exploited the market systematically. The Austrian company Containex, who supplied the containers for the Treehouse Trust nursery, deal in ordinary ISO shipping containers but also supply inhabitable units, for sale or hire, insulated, wired, plumbed and furnished. Walls are removable so that different linings and window configurations can be fitted in the factory, and whole sides can be omitted to make bigger internal

Container studios at Trinity Buoy Wharf by Nicolas Lacey.

Treehouse Trust by Penoyre and Prasad.

spaces. There is also a flat-pack version that comes with instructions for self-assembly. Hundreds of projects have been completed, including school classrooms, kindergartens, sports clubs, banks and an Antarctic research station, as well as routine temporary offices and workers' living accommodation. A total of 333 units were combined in a three-storey courtyard arrangement to create a complete temporary school in Woergl, Austria. It took less than two months to complete the building on site, including the erection of a separate umbrella roof. In Munich, a more elegant version of the 'containers-plus-umbrella-roof' idea, designed by architects Guggenbichler and Netzer, demonstrates how a few small refinements can convert a temporary municipal office building into something architectural magazines want to illustrate.

The offshore oil industry is an important user of containerized accommodation. Duffy and McGovern, based in Aberdeen, runs the world's largest fleet of A60 class 'cabins', which can be rented, leased or bought. There are two-person to twelve-person dormitories, all with en-suite showers and toilets; specialized engineering cabins fitted out as workshops, laboratories, control rooms and telephone exchanges; and general-purpose cabins, including offices, mini-galleys, mess rooms and laundries. All have to be built to very high safety standards. 'A60' indicates a one-hour fire resistance rating. Cabins are pressurized to prevent the build up of explosive gas and have to be 'started up' before they can be occupied. Nobody would expect the buildings on an oil rig to be 'architectural', but clusters of cabins stacked artlessly on crowded platforms in raging seas are the real-world counterparts of those Archigram fantasies of the 1960s. The inhabited parts of an oil rig constitute a high-tech working village of impressive variety and complexity. And it's all made out of containers.

But not all prefabricated, box-like buildings are adaptations of containers. Leaving aside the special case of the mobile home (see Chapter 3), modular construction has been used for many years for cellular buildings like hotels and student halls of residence. One fine, creative morning in the early 1980s, John Blyde and Peter Hutchinson, managing director and chairman of Potton, the Bedfordshire timber frame manufacturer, decided in one of their regular business brainstorming sessions that what Britain needed was an American-style budget hotel chain. Potton had been making modular housing units on a small scale for Basildon new town, but new planning guidelines (the famous Essex Design Guide) had begun to insist on a formally complex, neo-vernacular style that made modules uneconomic. Blyde and Hutchinson reasoned that a budget hotel in which every room was virtually identical was the perfect application for modular construction, and a chain of modular hotels might make their fortune. They built a prototype on a golf course owned by the company and invited representatives of eight of the country's most prominent hotel chains to inspect it. It was Forte that took the bait. Forte wanted to build small 'lodges' alongside their Little Chef roadside cafes. The target customer was the travelling businessman with a modest expense account who couldn't afford luxury but wanted an en-suite bathroom and a television. Most of all, he wanted reliability, a brand he knew he could trust, preferably identifiable from a moving car. In American terms, he wanted a good quality motel. Potton built the first Travelodge for Forte on the A38 just north of Birmingham in 1985 and hundreds more followed over the next fifteen years.

The typical early Travelodge was a simple linear building, two storeys high, with a minimal reception area and double-loaded corridors serving 40 identical rooms. The basic product was not the hotel, but the individual room, and with

Travelodge Hotel.

Forte developing five or six sites at any one time there was ample scope for standardization and prefabrication. Potton adapted its production line to produce stout wooden boxes and fit them out with everything you would expect in a well-equipped hotel room, from the sanitary fittings in the bathroom to the pictures on the wall. When the room was finished, the door was locked shut, not to be opened again until the chamber-maid arrived with the sheets. The box was then shrink-wrapped, transported to the site, lifted into position by crane, roofed over and walled in. External walls and roofs varied according to the whims of local development control officers who fondly imagined that a brickwork skin, a concrete-tiled roof, a scattering of gables and a fake dovecote could make a motel look like a manor house. But the architects employed to design the site layout and prepare the planning drawings were in no position to object and the client didn't mind as long as the building programme was not delayed. The architectural banality of the Travelodge literally obscured its technical achievement. Prefabrication meant that the rooms could be manufactured while the site was being prepared and the whole process typically took only sixteen weeks. This was not just an experimental prototype but the commercially successful application of factory production to a nationwide building programme.

The pace of motel building in Britain has slackened in recent years as the supply of suitable roadside sites has dried up. Potton has gone back to its core business of providing timber-frame houses for the self-build market and John Blyde is now a building systems consultant. But the big hotel and leisure companies are still on the look out for building systems that can save them time and money. Room modules are now usually framed in light steel rather than timber, and manufacturers like Terrapin and Britspace, with wider client bases, have entered the field. Concrete has made a comeback too. Bell and Webster, of Grantham in Lincolnshire, market a pre-cast panel system called

Fast Build Rooms that is not too different in principle from the old mass housing systems of the 1960s. Rooms arrive on the site as flat packs of structural floor and wall panels, their interior surfaces ready for decoration and carpeting. Customers include the Ibis, Holiday Inn and Ramada hotel chains, but the biggest project to date is a 1,601-bedroom student housing complex for the University of Hertfordshire.

If hotels and halls of residence (not to mention barracks and prisons) can be prefabricated in flat-pack or modular form, then why not ordinary apartments for single people and couples, in particular those 'keyworkers' – nurses, policemen, teachers – who can't afford to house themselves close to their city workplaces? London architects Piercy Conner attracted the attention of the mainstream media in 2001 with their speculative design for a 'Microflat', a 25-square-metre (269 sq ft) modular living unit designed with keyworkers in mind. Just giving it a catchy name was enough to save the press release from the newsroom wastepaper bin; presenting it as an urban crash pad for young professionals rather than, say, a hostel for penniless nurses did the rest. There was talk of 'caravan and yacht technology', Jonathan Glancey of the *Guardian* newspaper compared the concept to Kisho Kurokawa's Nagakin Capsule Tower of 1972,[1] and before long Selfridges department store had put one in its Oxford Street window, complete with live inhabitants. Getting a real one built was not so easy, partly because, as the architects themselves admitted, developers prefer not to put large sums of money into the hands of young architects. Other reasons might have been that the Microflat was too expensive and the only thing that was new about it, apart from the multi-media website, was a slight kink in the plan to create a modelled façade and an attractive angled balcony. Otherwise it was essentially a motel room or a student bed-sit.

Meanwhile bigger companies with lower profiles get on with the real business of providing accommodation for students and keyworkers. For example, Unite, which supplies comprehensive property services to universities and National Health Service Trusts, routinely uses modular prefabricated en-suite rooms in all its new-build projects. In 2002 it opened a new 18,000-square-metre automated factory in Stonehouse, Gloucestershire, which claims to produce fully fitted modules at the rate of one every 22 minutes. Regional teams of 'architects', unnamed in the promotional literature, draw up plans on the basis of a technical and design manual, with rooms arranged in clusters around fully fitted kitchens. The results are architecturally undistinguished, but the big attraction for clients is that this is a complete package, including management, maintenance and rent collection.

Even if the bedrooms are not modularized, it often makes sense to modularize the bathrooms. In a now distant echo of the language of Archigram,

Microflats by Piercy Conner, computer generated collage.

everyone calls prefabricated bathrooms 'pods'. The famous historical example, of course, is Buckminster Fuller's Dymaxion Bathroom of 1936 for the
Phelps-Dodge Copper Company, although it never went into production and
architectural historians tend to forget that it was only one of several modular
bathroom designs for which patents were sought at that time. A more recent
precedent, Nicholas Grimshaw's International Students' Club service tower

(1967) in London, is famous as one of the two buildings that inaugurated the British High Tech style, the other being the Reliance Controls Factory in Swindon by Team 4 (Richard Rogers and Norman Foster) of the same year. While his then partner Terry Farrell converted the existing nineteenth-century building into student bed-sits, Grimshaw set about spending most of the budget on glass-fibre bathroom pods that spiralled round a pipe duct in a glass-clad cylindrical tower. It was a daring concept, but disastrous in practice. Cantilevered lavatory pans broke off in use, no one knew how to mend them and before long the students were having to get used to a different kind of prefabricated toilet set up temporarily in the garden.[2]

Twenty years later, that masterpiece of the High Tech style, the Lloyd's Building in London, designed by Richard Rogers, used prefabricated toilet pods displayed prominently on the outside of the building. Like shiny stainless-steel containers stacked in a concrete storage rack, they look as though they are designed to be replaced when they wear out. This is a typical High Tech idea, conceptually elegant and visually striking but almost impossible to achieve in practice. In fact the pods were fixed on the rack as it was built, floor by floor, and they would be very hard to remove. But perhaps this question of unplugability is a red herring, an imaginary scenario invented by High Tech architects looking for reasons to make their buildings look dynamic and indeterminate. There are plenty of ordinary practical reasons for assembling the most heavily serviced parts of buildings in factories and carrying them to the site in boxes. First it saves time by overlapping the on-site and in-factory production processes. The frame of the building can be going up while the pods are being manufactured. Second, it improves the quality of the product. It is much easier to install sanitary fittings in a warm, dry factory with all the tools to hand than it is to do it on the draughty, wet, untidy and ill-equipped upper floor of a half-finished building. Third, since the pod in the factory is accessible all round and can be got at from any angle, mechanical plant, pipework and ductwork can be installed much more compactly.

The building industry did not need any architectural theory to convince it of these advantages, and many British companies now make and market bathroom pods, often framed in light steel. Farquhar, based in Huntly, Grampian, produces about 4,000 pods a year, ranging from small shower cubicles for student accommodation to big executive washrooms. They almost never become part of a building's architecture, at least not externally. Washrooms for multi-storey office buildings are simply lifted in at the appropriate level through a hole in the external wall and slid into position on the floor ready for plumbing and wiring in. The door stays locked shut until all danger of damage to the

Lloyds Building toilet pods.

expensive finishes and fittings by burly builders has passed. Pods are often imported from continental Europe, Denmark being a particular centre of pod expertise. E. J. Badekabiner of Hedensted supplied pre-cast concrete bathroom pods for Montevetro, a luxury riverside apartment block in London designed by Richard Rogers. But the company also supplies the budget hotel chain Holiday Inn Express.

Biro, Thermos, Hoover, Tannoy: some brand names are too successful for their own good. Portakabin is one such, having become more of a nuisance than a benefit to the company that coined it. Portakabin was founded in 1961 by Donald Shepherd, chairman of Shepherd Construction, on the basis of an idea for instant site huts. The idea was made practicable, however, by an architect, Reg Stallard, who had worked on the famous Hertfordshire Schools programme.[3] At that time Shepherd Construction made plywood cement silos that were becoming obsolete with the coming of ready mixed concrete. In a classic case of technology transfer, Stallard adapted this silo operation, in particular the ability to make seamless scarf joints, to the assembly of inhabitable plywood boxes. The original Portakabin was 16 by 7 ft (4.88 by 2.13 metres), with continuous plywood sides and ingenious telescopic legs that enabled it to be unloaded from a flatbed lorry by just one person. The direct descendant of this little building is the model now called Pacemaker. With its bright yellow doors and round-cornered windows it has become something of a design classic and is much imitated. Pacemakers come in different lengths and widths, and can be linked together and stacked up. They have slightly larger cousins called Pullman and Titan, and there is an open-sided modular system called Duplex to create bigger interior spaces. But all are temporary and relocateable. When the company wanted to expand into the permanent prefabricated building market it had to get rid of the Portakabin brand name. The result was Yorkon, a system based on steel-framed modules but flexible enough to be used for almost any building type. Curiously, though it takes its share of hotel chain business, Yorkon has never, until very recently, shown much interest in housing. Although inventive and adventurous in other fields, the firm has never done the obvious thing and marketed a Portakabin designed to be lived in.

Not, that is, until 1998 when Dickon Robinson, the development director of the Peabody Trust, decided it was time to commission a modular prefabricated housing scheme for London keyworkers. Peabody is itself a well-known brand. Founded in 1862 to house London's poor with a £500,000 bequest from an American banker, George Peabody, it now manages a portfolio of 17,000 homes. Londoners associate the name with a particular type of late nineteenth-century tenement block. It was these sturdy, well-designed buildings, many still in use and popular with tenants, that inspired Robinson to become an architectural patron and not just a housing bureaucrat. The site chosen for the innovative new housing scheme was in inner East London, among the warehouses and council housing blocks of Hoxton, on the corner of Shepherdess Walk and Murray Grove. Murray Grove was the name that stuck, a name that was soon to become famous in the world of housing and construction. Cartwright Pickard were chosen as architects after a limited competition,

Murray Grove Housing by Cartwright Pickard.

and Yorkon were selected as module manufacturer at an early stage so that designers and makers could work together.

The building is a simple, L-shaped block, five storeys high, with a cylindrical stair and lift tower in the recessed corner, access decks on the street frontages and balconies overlooking a garden at the back. Seventy four light steel-framed modules, fully fitted out and finished internally, arrived at the site two per lorry. It took just ten days (two five-day phases) to crane them into position on the prepared foundations. Already the building was topped out and watertight. After that there were delays. Twelve weeks were lost during the fitting of the decks, balconies, stair tower, roof and external cladding, and by hand-over day the programme had slipped a total of seventeen weeks. When compared with a similar but traditionally built Peabody building nearby, Murray Grove was a little quicker (44 weeks as against 62 weeks) and slightly more expensive.[4] On balance a good performance for a client and an architect new to modular construction, but hardly a triumph. Why then did it become famous? One reason was that it was a handsome and photogenic piece of architecture. James Pickard and Peter Cartwright had very respectable architectural pedigrees, having worked for many years in the offices of Peter Foggo and Michael Hopkins respectively. This showed in the neat detailing of Murray Grove and in certain features such as the very Hopkins-like stair tower. Yorkon could easily have answered the same brief with a routine design-build job clad in brickwork. The technology would have been essentially the same and it would almost certainly have been cheaper, but nobody would have taken any notice, least of all the architectural magazines.

But there was another, more important reason why Murray Grove was quickly established as a milestone project. In July 1998 the government's Construction Task Force chaired by Sir John Egan, the ex-boss of Jaguar cars and the British Airports Authority, had published its findings. *Rethinking Construction*, better known as the Egan Report,[5] called upon Britain's poorly equipped and inefficient construction industry to put its own house in order, to stop tearing itself apart in wasteful competitive tendering procedures and to begin co-operating, or 'partnering', to provide a better service for its customers. It could do this, said the report, by adopting the methods of modern manufacturing industry. Why, asked Sir John, in yet another utterance of that call that echoes down the twentieth century, couldn't buildings be made like motor cars? Murray Grove was the perfect standard-bearer for the new vision of construction as an efficient manufacturing industry. It was in London where all the important people could see it, it was architect designed, it had been commissioned by a well-known social housing provider, and it was modular, so the publicity material could include that essential shot of a module being hoisted aloft by a crane.

In the flurry of technical literature that followed in the wake of the Egan Report, every case study, every demonstration project report, every technical journal article about prefabrication, every quasi-governmental construction website included a mention of Murray Grove, usually in the first paragraph. Cartwright Pickard, firmly established as modular pioneers, went on to design a similar scheme called Sixth Avenue for a housing association in York. The Peabody Trust commissioned another young London architectural practice, Allford, Hall, Monaghan and Morris (AHMM), to design a bigger version, with staggered modules to create integral balconies, on the Raines Dairy site in Stoke Newington. Yorkon was the module maker in both cases. British modular construction had come a long way since those early timber Travelodges. Architecture had made it respectable.

And yet from a technical, theoretical or even historical point of view, it is hard to get excited about these modular social housing projects. They represent a reforging of the old alliance between the architectural profession, public money and new forms of construction, and they suffer from the old delusions.

Raines Dairy housing by AHMM.

Their technology is actually rather primitive, offering no immediate advantage over conventional construction for either client or builder. Yorkon's factory is no high tech marvel. Basic module shells are made on an assembly line under cover, but the internal fitting out takes place in an open yard, tidier but not much better equipped than a low-density building site.

Architecturally Murray Grove, Raines Dairy and Sixth Avenue are fine buildings, but from the tenants' or owner-occupiers' point of view they are just modern blocks of flats, no different from thousands of others. The first tenants of Murray Grove were very happy with their flats, especially with the build quality, but it was only the media mentions and the flocks of visitors (amusing to some, irritating to others) that made them aware of the building's unusual construction. If this represents a revolution in social housing it is one that is virtually invisible to its consumers. Where is the flexibility and choice, the customization that modern production and marketing are supposed to offer? Would it matter if someone decided to paint the outside of their flat a different colour, or fit a neo-Georgian door, or build a conservatory on the balcony? How do these buildings deal with that old conflict between individual and collective form, a problem that Le Corbusier was aware of back in 1925 when he tried to market the apartments of his Immeubles Villas project as free-standing houses? It seems perverse to make dwellings in a factory as independent portable structures but

Royal Northern College of Music halls of residence, Manchester.

'm-house' designed by mae architects.

Omar park home; the Sheringham.

then only offer them as identical apartments fixed permanently in multi-storey blocks. And there is still a tendency to reinvent the product for every site, even when the client and manufacturer (Peabody and Yorkon) are the same. A different architect inevitably means a different module, or a different way of using modules: add-on versus integrated balconies, for example. Traditional architectural authorship still exerts its conservative influence. A closer, longer-term relationship between designer and manufacturer might result in the development of a truly useful range of modular products for a real market.

Commercial companies like Unite and the budget hotel chains ignore the architectural obstacle and as a result they make the running, technically and commercially, if not architecturally. In 2001 a modular hall of residence was completed in Manchester for the Royal Northern College of Music. It was designed by modular specialists, Design Buro, working with manufacturers Rollalong and Ayrshire Metal Products. It was built to a tight timetable and a tough budget under the government's Private Finance Initiative. At nine storeys, it is the world's tallest modular building outside the US, yet hardly anyone in the architectural profession has heard of it. It is the familiar story. The architect-designed, one-off project gets the publicity and enters the history books, while the despised commercial operators quietly get on with the serious business of technical innovation and volume production.

Eventually, of course, architects adopt the innovations and claim them as their own. There is no shortage of architect-designed prototypes for container houses: a two-module summer house in Iceland by Glama-Kim Arkitektar; the LV Home, a vacation cabin designed by the Chilean architect Rocio Romero for her parents; a couple of interesting mobile boxes, the FRED and the SU-SI, by the Austrian practice KFN Systems; and many more.[6] There is no sign of any of them becoming commercially viable products. In September 2002 architect and exhibition designer Tim Pyne launched a new concept in individual modular homes called the 'm-house'. Designed by mae architects, It was a simple single-storey box made in two halves out of plywood and timber studs. Each half had a steel chassis and wheels so that it could be towed to the site. There was a choice of external cladding – cedar boarding or profiled metal – which was taken up as a parapet to hide a valley roof. Details like porch decks to hide the wheels and full-height windows with external shading devices gave it a neat, designer look. Photomontages were published showing the m-house in various locations: on a beach, in a big garden as a granny flat, on the roof of an old industrial building, on a pontoon in a river. It was, of course, nothing more than a restyled mobile home. In Britain mobile homes are called caravans if their wheels are still visible and 'park homes' if they have pitched roofs and other features reminiscent of permanent housing. Like their bigger and more developed American cousins, and as their name suggests, they are often gathered together in gated communities for retired people.

Restyling and rebranding the park home to make it attractive to younger buyers was not a bad idea, but it was hardly a new housing concept. Six months after the launch Pyne had sold precisely one m-house – not much of a challenge to the established park home manufacturers. Omar Homes Limited of Brandon in Suffolk, for example, offer a choice of fourteen different models, with names like Heritage, Sheringham and Ashdale, and 60 different floor plans, plus lots of optional extras like dormers, porches and Tudor beams. None of them will ever be featured in a design magazine. Or try the mobile homes produced by Norwegian Log Chalets of Reading for an unbeatable combination of solidity and mobility, prefabrication and craftsmanship, modernity and tradition: 'No cladding, no boarding, just real solid log all the way through.'

# 9. The robot and the carpenter

We arrive by car, having made our way slowly along narrow roads between rice fields on the final leg of the journey. We are in Shiga Prefecture, about 64 kilometres (40 miles) north-east of Osaka. The manager of the National Panahome factory welcomes us with a smile and a joke as we sit down for tea at the meeting table in his modestly appointed office. The chief researcher and the production manager are in attendance. They all wear uniform, not suits and ties but clean, ironed, beige and grey overalls with matching baseball caps. The factory consists of several large sheds, interspersed with car parks, service yards and a surprising number of mature trees. Everything is clean, tidy and new-looking, the sheds as smart as the two-tone overalls, which we now see are worn by all the workers. First we are to be shown the main production line for external walls. It is almost 200 metres long, occupying one side of a brightly lit shed, which has a pale blue floor and white-painted steelwork. As we walk along a generous visitors' gangway, separated from the production line by a stout steel safety rail, we have the benefit of a running commentary through our headphones. What is described to us and what we see is an assembly process hardly less automated than that of the most advanced car manufacturer.

Wall frames of light welded steel, laid horizontally, glide slowly along the track, pausing at each computer-controlled machine to receive a sub-component or undergo a fixing operation. Glue is squirted in ranks of identical dollops, never missing the constantly shifting target. Pre-cut gypsum boards are lifted from piles by giant suckers and lowered into position, accurate to the millimetre. Gangs of drill bits dip and rise. Screws filter down their feed pipes to the multiple screw drivers. Halfway down the track, the panel is automatically turned over to receive its infill of insulation and its external cladding of 10-mm thick, storey-height, composite plastic sheet, the opening for a window already cut. A few workers stand by to keep an eye on the robots, but they hardly ever intervene, and it's the same for all the other processes in the factory – fitting, cutting, bending, welding, riveting, nailing, spraying. When a panel

National Panahome factory interior.

reaches the end of the line a robot lowers it onto a conveyor beneath the main
track and sends it back to the start, where it is transferred to a second track to
receive secondary components like windows and doors. Every panel is different, and yet the right window frame for this particular panel is always the next
one hanging from the overhead conveyor.

Yes, every panel is different. Our guide glances at a bar-coded label. This
panel is for Mr Sato's house – a four-bedroom luxury detached house for a site
in an outer suburb of Osaka. When the panel is finished it will be shrink-
wrapped and loaded onto one of six trucks containing all the wall, floor and
roof panels for Mr Sato's house. The six trucks will make up the first of three
deliveries to the site. The next delivery will be a single truck-load of secondary
elements like the staircase and the balcony. The final truck will contain finish-
ing touches like light fittings, taps and soap dishes. Mr Sato ordered his house
four weeks ago. It will take about eight weeks to complete it on site.

National Panahome has eight factories like the one in Shiga Prefecture. The
company makes about 10,000 detached houses a year and is one of the 'big five'
Japanese prefabricated housing manufacturers. The others are Sekisui House,
Sekisui Heim, Daiwa and Misawa. Their products and manufacturing methods
vary quite widely. Daiwa's factory near Nara, for example, is much less automated than Panahome's Shiga plant. Both produce similar steel-framed wall
panels, but the Daiwa tracks are lined with workers positioning components by
hand and wielding electric and pneumatic hand tools for drilling, nailing, gluing

and screwing. These workers are not directly employed by Daiwa, but are members of subcontract labour gangs. A big digital display panel hangs over each track showing the performance targets and production rates. Sekisui Heim markets a modular system. Houses are assembled from steel- or timber-framed, room-size boxes. Electrical wiring, pipework assemblies, sanitary fittings, kitchen cupboards, bathroom 'pods', staircases, ironmongery – all are fitted in the factory. Modularization halves the on-site assembly time of other prefabricated systems. Each house consists of ten to fifteen modules, which are delivered to the site on purpose-made low-loader trucks. Six men and a crane complete the basic unit assembly in just four hours.

Japan's population is roughly twice that of the UK, but it builds about six times as much new housing every year. Houses are seen as consumer goods rather than financial investments and are expected to last an average of only 26 years. A Japanese family that wants a new house will often simply pull down the house it is living in and have the new house built on the same site. Sekisui Heim offers a special deal for house replacement: a maximum 50-day period (including weekends) from moving out of the old house to moving into the new one. Planning restrictions are usually limited to zoning, density and height. Detailed site planning and external appearance are not controlled. Of course many Japanese families live in apartments, especially in the big cities, but almost half of new housing completions are detached houses. About three-quarters of these are individually commissioned, and almost one third of these are prefabricated. That adds up to about 120,000 factory-made houses per year.[1]

For almost a century, European and American architects and builders have dreamt of the factory-made house, the house that is made and marketed like a motor car. In Japan the dream has come true. What is more, all the supposed disadvantages of mass production – the standardization, the monotony, the lack of choice – have turned out to be illusions. Japanese prefabricated house builders all share two basic aims: to give customers exactly what they want, and to avoid all unnecessary waste in the production process. Customization and 'lean production' are taken for granted.

One floor of a large office block in northern Osaka has been converted into what National Panahomes calls its 'Human Plaza'. It is, in effect, the shop where customers buy their houses. There is a cinema, or rather a luxurious lounge in which promotional videos are shown, and a large exhibition of kitchens, bathrooms and full-size mock-ups of substantial pieces of house, cut away to show the high levels of insulation and the earthquake-proof construction. Eventually, potential clients are persuaded to sit down with a designer/salesman to choose their house and agree any modifications to the standard type. But the concept of a standard type is misleading. Standard types only exist in the company's brochures, catalogues and web pages. They are a useful starting point for a design discussion but they are not necessary for the organization of the manufacturing process. The houses as built are all different. Of course, they have to be designed within the limits of a constructional method – timber frame or steel frame, panel-based or modular – and the manufacturing plant can only deal with curtain types of material (it can't, for example, build brick walls) but the 'system' allows infinite permutations of plan, finish and interior fit-out. The design discussion used to be facilitated by two-dimensional drawings and physical models. Now it's all done in virtual reality. The customer would like a gable roof instead of a hip roof? No problem. A few mouse clicks and it appears. Constructional modifications will be dealt with later. A larger balcony? A smaller porch? An extra bedroom? Eventually, perhaps after several meetings, the unique design is finalized. It will take perhaps two days to make those constructional modifications on the computer system and produce the production drawings and schedules. Materials and components will be ordered automatically from an established chain of suppliers. They will arrive 'just in time' to be assembled in the factory on machinery that receives its instructions from the same computer system.

Daiwa's equivalent of the 'Human Plaza' is larger and more elaborate. It is housed in a handsome, four-storey building on the same site as the company's central research laboratory in the Heijo-Soraku district of Kansai Science City. In addition to the usual marketing suite, there is a 'commemorative' exhibition of the company's history. Daiwa was founded soon after the Second World War by Nobuo Ishibashi who, now in his eighties, is still listed as a senior adviser to the company. The first product line was a tiny metal garden shed designed to provide schoolchildren living in cramped, multi-occupied houses

Daiwa's first product line.

Daiwa's prototype testing laboratory.

with space in which to do their homework. Two surviving examples are included in the exhibition as well as dozens of scale models to illustrate 50 years of prefabricated house production. The company has in recent years tried to improve its image by stressing the environmental friendliness of its products, so on another floor there is a large museum of 'Environmental Symbiosis Houses of the World' including models and mock-ups of yurts, tepees, Indonesian long houses and the like.

'Environmental Symbiosis' is one of those 'Janglish' slogans that are such an essential part of any Japanese marketing campaign. It supposedly sums up the ethos of the research laboratory, which is equipped to test every conceivable technical aspect of domestic construction. Full-size prototypes are buffeted by artificial wind, sprayed by artificial rain, baked or frozen by artificial weather and shaken on the earthquake test table. Materials are set on fire in the fire resistance lab and mock-ups of interiors are tested in the lighting and acoustics labs. Outside in the forecourt of the complex stands the Environmental Symbiosis show house in which various environmentally friendly features are demonstrated: a conservatory, a wind catcher, an array of solar collectors, a ceiling radiation air-conditioning system. Next door stands the Lifelong Active Dwelling, another experimental house designed for the elderly and infirm.

Show houses are often built on factory sites. National Panahomes, for example, has found room for a whole suburban cul-de-sac on its Shiga site. Visitors to the show houses are also invited to tour the factory, which is one reason why it is always clean and tidy. It is all part of the effort to promote brand loyalty, a concept that has a special potency in Japan. Customers for prefabricated houses are interested in more than just the product and the price. They are also interested in the process, the way the product is made and marketed and the image the company projects. In some ways this is perfectly rational. Designer/salesmen really do ensure that customers get exactly what they want and the production, delivery and erection of the house really is a fast, efficient operation. The house itself is a genuinely high-quality product and most companies provide a comprehensive after-sales service. But there is also an irrational aspect to this relationship between company and customer. Customers are more like participants than punters and they seem to take a pride in their participation, almost as if they were employees of the company. Those Daiwa research laboratories are not just well equipped, they are excessively well equipped. They would not disgrace a national building research centre. And yet most of the big companies maintain similar facilities. The technology of automated prefabrication might be advanced when compared with traditional building construction, but the final product is, after all, only a house, not a jet aeroplane. How many times does a house need to be wind tunnel tested? There is no doubt that genuine research and development does take place in these laboratories but they are also 'customer orientated'. In other words, they are as much part of the marketing effort as the showrooms, video lounges and educational exhibitions. They are there to impress, to instil pride and loyalty in workers and customers alike.

How do customers identify a brand to be loyal to? Through advertising, of course, on billboards, on television and radio, on the Web and in newspapers. But a better way to shop for a house is to visit a show village, like the Senri Housing Park in northern Osaka. The park is operated by the broadcasting company ABC. Individual plots for show houses are let to house manufacturers on five-year leases. There are about 50 show houses at Senri, which is the largest of about 400 show villages in Japan. More than 20,000 families visit the park every year, comparing the products of about 30 manufacturers. The site is laid out like a quiet suburb and the effect is remarkably realistic. Sales staff are on hand in every house and visitors undertaking serious comparative research quickly collect several carrier bags full of brochures. Some of the brochures are like works of art – 30-page large-format coffee-table books with vast and perfect colour photographs printed on heavy sumptuous paper. In another context the page layouts and typography would win publishing awards. If these were architectural monographs, you would pay £50 each for them. And then there are the comprehensive technical brochures. Sekisui Heim, for example, produce an 84-page, larger -than-A3, perfect-bound paper-

Senri Housing Park, Osaka.

back called, simply, *Unit Technology*. There are chapters on earthquake resistance, energy conservation, fire proofing, acoustics, disabled access and every other technical aspect of domestic building construction. It includes plans, axonometrics, large-scale details, maps, graphs, tables, bar charts and diagrams – all in colour and all laid out with educational clarity to explain difficult technical concepts to lay people. If it were not for an understandable emphasis on the advantages of Sekisui Heim's modular system, this brochure would make a very good textbook for first-year architecture students. There are even brochures specifically about the factories, illustrated with photographs of pristine machinery, taken with loving care.

The customers for Japanese prefabricated houses, then, are not so much buying a product as buying into a brand image, associating themselves with a successful company. It is hard not to be impressed, as the customers are, by the efficiency of the whole operation. But equally, for an architect at least, it is hard not to be disappointed by the houses themselves. A quick tour round the Senri park confirms a growing suspicion that, despite all the differences of material and method between one manufacturer and another, the houses all end up looking the same: two-storey, detached, with pitched roofs, either hipped or gabled, and various projecting bays, porches and balconies, arranged picturesquely but without much evidence of design logic. Inside, the plans are mostly utterly conventional: living-room, dining-room, kitchen and three bedrooms. Such character as these houses have comes from an unquestioning conformity to a globally recognizable image of suburban luxury. One common feature puts them irrevocably beyond the architectural pale: plastic cladding, textured to look like brick. And this in a country with no tradition of brick construction.

Here we have the taste problem in a nutshell. Everything is right about Japanese prefabricated housing, or at least everything that most people consider important – the quality, the efficiency, the customer satisfaction. But most architects, that tiny minority of the population that subscribes to a different set of aesthetic values, will dismiss these products with no more than a quick glance and contemptuous grimace. Of course this is of little concern to the manufacturers, who are simply giving the customers what they want, or perhaps what they have been persuaded to want. Why should it matter what architects think? Architects dislike many products of the building industry, especially those produced without the help of architects. But in this particular case the architects' regret and disappointment is perhaps understandable. The reason is that the Japanese detached house, in its old, traditional, vernacular form, is a kind of architectural paragon. Twentieth-century western architects, especially the Modernists, were besotted with the Japanese house, even though no architect had ever had any influence on it over the centuries of its evolution.

Consider some of the qualities of the traditional Japanese house. It is asymmetrical and indeterminate. Its plan is simple, extendable and modular (in the standard dimension sense), the dimensions of each room being determined by the six feet by three feet *tatami* mats that form its floor. The structure is timber post-and-beam, the floor is raised off the ground and the walls are non-load-bearing. There are few windows or doors, in the sense of holes in the wall. Instead whole sections of wall, both internal and external, take the form of lightweight, sliding, paper-covered panels, called *shoji* if translucent and *fusuma* if opaque. These panels can be removed completely to create larger spaces or to open up the interior to the garden. Inside and outside, house and garden, merge on the verandah. With its walls removed, the house is reduced to its most characteristic and essential element: the big, overhanging, all-embracing roof. Though mostly unadorned, these houses are nevertheless aesthetically extremely subtle, relying for their effect on proportion and scale, light and shade, and on the intrinsic qualities of natural materials, above all unpainted wood in all its inexhaustible variety. The space is uncluttered because there is no furniture in the western sense, no beds or chairs, only futons and cushions stored in built-in cupboards when not in use. It is easy to see why early modernist architects in Europe and America, looking for a lighter, simpler, less formal alternative to the classical and Gothic traditions, should have fallen in love with the Japanese house.

Illustrations from *Japanese Homes and their Surroundings*, by Edward S. Morse.

In 1877 Edward S. Morse, an American biologist and illustrator, was appointed Professor of Zoology at Tokyo Imperial University. He seems, however, to have spent most of his time in Japan studying houses rather than animals and is mainly remembered now as the author of *Japanese Homes and their Surroundings*, which was published in Boston in 1885. Morse brought a scientist's analytical eye to his subject and applied his skills as an illustrator in a set of beautiful line drawings. His aim was to compile a verbal and visual record of the Japanese house before it was destroyed by the steamroller of westernization. The book is still widely available in facsimile editions and remains the best detailed description in English of the traditional Japanese house.[2] While Morse was at the Imperial University, he managed to secure a position as Professor of Philosophy and Political Economy for an old Boston friend, Edward F.

Ward W. Willits house by Frank Lloyd Wright.

Fenellosa. Fenellosa was also deflected from his official duties by a growing love of traditional Japanese art and culture, and when he returned to the United States in 1890 he became curator of the Japanese department of the Boston Museum of Fine Arts. Fenellosa's cousin, Joseph L. Silsbee, was an architect in Chicago; one of Silsbee's employees, for just a few months in 1887, was Frank Lloyd Wright, then eighteen years old and at the very start of a career that would eventually earn him the undisputed title of America's greatest architect.

The evidence is circumstantial, but there is little reason to question historian Kevin Nute's opinion that, seven years before he saw the Japanese exhibits at the 1893 World's Columbian Exhibition in Chicago and twenty years before his first visit to Japan, Wright must have been familiar with the traditional Japanese house through Edward Morse's book.[3] Architectural historians argue about the extent of the influence of the Japanese architecture on Wright's mature style. In the great 'Prairie houses', from the Ward W. Willits house of 1902 to the Robie House of 1909, the resemblance seems perfectly clear – the asymmetrical plans, the dominant overhanging roofs, the verandahs and the window-walls. The trouble is that Wright himself consistently denied that his buildings were in any way influenced by the Japanese house. For many years he collected Japanese prints, becoming one of the most important dealers in America and often making more money from this business than from his architectural practice. He was quite willing to acknowledge the indirect influence on his work of the bold, spare art of Hokusai or Hiroshige, but he could never bring himself to share the credit for his creations with any other architect, not even with a centuries-old architectural tradition:

My work is original not only in fact but in spiritual fiber. No practice by any European architect to this day has influenced mine in the least. As for the Incas, the Mayans, even the Japanese – all were to me but splendid confirmation.[4]

It is the authentic, original voice of architectural arrogance. Wright's was perhaps the first modern architecture to show the clear influence of the traditional Japanese house, but the image so vividly encapsulated by Edward Morse was to remain influential throughout the twentieth century. For Mies van der Rohe the lesson of Japan was in the clear separation of load-bearing frame and non-load-bearing wall. The German modernist Bruno Taut, no longer welcome in Nazi Germany, went to live in Japan for a time in the 1930s and wrote a book about his experiences there called *Houses and People of Japan*.[5] Taut acknowledged a debt to Edward Morse and also to Tetsuro Yoshida, whose book *Das Japanische Wohnhaus*, published in 1935, was written at the suggestion of two other German modernists, Hugo Häring and Ludwig Hilberseimer. In the 1950s Tetsuro's well-illustrated book was revised and translated into English, ensuring the continued influence of the Japanese house on the post-war generation.[6] In 1954 Walter Gropius made an extended visit to Japan. Ten years later he wrote this:

Of course many of its features that seem related to our western architecture have developed from entirely different premises. But our modern architectural requirements of simplicity, of outdoor-indoor relation, of flexibility, of modular co-ordination and prefabrication, and, most importantly, of variety of expression, have found such fascinating answers in the classic domestic architecture of Japan that no architect should neglect its stimulating study.[7]

Western architects have tended to see one feature of the Japanese house – its apparent modular co-ordination – as especially relevant to the development of architecture in an industrial society. For most of the twentieth century it was assumed that the standardization and co-ordination of dimensions was a necessary precondition for the efficient mass production of building components. Japanese domestic architecture seemed to provide the perfect example of a complete building system in which the size of every column, beam, panel, joist and rafter was governed by fixed geometrical rules. In his influential book *The Japanese House*, published in 1964, Heinrich Engel described the Japanese Kiwari modular system as 'a definite challenge to any modular system of contemporary architecture. The order encompasses the wooden architecture of the entire nation.'[8] Engel devoted a chapter of his book to a detailed graphic

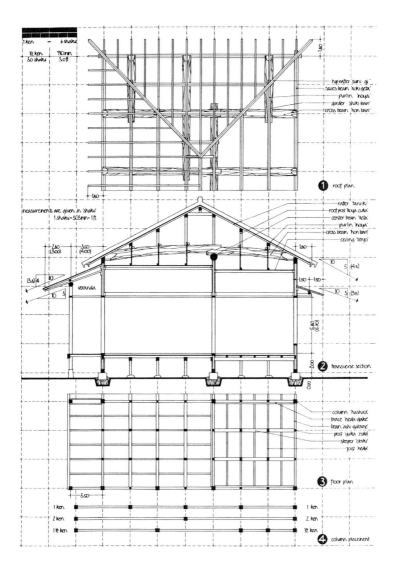

The modular order of the Japanese house, from Heinrich Engel's *The Japanese House*.

analysis of the order of Kiwari. What emerges is a very simple system based on the Ken, a standard dimension for the spacing of columns, divided into either 6 or 6.5 Shaku, or feet. (The discrepancy arises because of two different ways of measuring the distance between columns – centreline to centreline, or face to face.) There are further subdivisions and sub-subdivisions using an ingenious combination of decimal and duodecimal arithmetic. The idea that this system was applied with almost complete consistency across 'an entire nation' was deeply satisfying to modernist architects trying to develop an architecture suitable for factory production.

Like most timber-framed structures, the building of a traditional Japanese house involved a degree of prefabrication. From the middle of the eighteenth century timber sizes began to be standardized and components such as *tatami* mats and *shoji* screens were manufactured in bulk in specialist workshops. But to see the order of Kiwari simply as a proto-industrial process is arguably a completely false interpretation. Regularity and repetition are features of most architectural traditions and only rarely are they motivated by the efficient production of building components. The columns of the Parthenon are apparently identical, but each was carved separately by hand. Dimensional systems in architecture are more often interpreted in spiritual or cosmological terms – the harmonic proportions of a Brunelleschi church, for example, seen as a representation of the harmony of the universe (see Chapter 6). Kiwari in its practical, domestic form, was a development of earlier, more complex proportional systems used in the construction of Buddhist temples and monasteries. There is also, perhaps, a social and political explanation for what Engel, in his enthusiasm, calls 'a modular order unique in the history of world architecture'. The Tokugawa shogunate that ruled Japan during the Edo period, from the early seventeenth century until 1868, was extremely restrictive and bureaucratic, regulating every aspect of the behaviour of its subjects. Standard house types for each social class were specified in great detail and enforced by law. The Kiwari system was therefore just one aspect of a general habit of social conformity and a mistrust of individuality.

The Kiwari system was passed down from generation to generation in documents such as the Shomei scrolls of 1608, the earliest surviving example of a Japanese carpenter's manual. By the middle of the eighteenth century manuals were being wood-block printed. Some were like pattern books, containing suggestions for house plans, others set out three-dimensional scale drawings of every conceivable carpenter's joint. The carpenter therefore, though a consummate craftsman, was not in any sense a designer. The layout of a proposed house would be decided by the client, who was just as familiar with the planning rules as the carpenter. The carpenter would then sketch out a simplified plan, decide the spacing of columns and the form of the roof according to custom, and select the constructional details from the standard repertoire. Traditional prototypes took the place of both spatial and technical design. Invention played no part. It is ironic that architects should be so in thrall to the traditional Japanese house, which, in its anonymity and its resistance to novelty, seems to represent the opposite of everything architecture stands for. It was the epitome of good taste and yet it was appreciated by a whole society, not just a privileged élite. It was a work of art, yet no artist was involved in its production, only the carpenter through which tradition acted. In short it was 'vernacular'. Architects, by definition, cannot do vernacular, they can only observe it, admire it and try to learn from it. It is the state of innocence from which architecture has lapsed irrevocably.

There really is no need to explain the Kiwari system, or any other aspect of the Japanese house, in social, political, spiritual or aesthetic, let alone industrial terms. On one level it was simply a practical arrangement, a settled way of doing things that saved time and avoided argument, resulting in economical, inoffensive buildings. But at another level, because it was traditional, because it was a language, given not invented, it also embodied the very soul of Japanese society. There is much in the traditional Japanese house that must remain mysterious to a westerner. Most westerners find it difficult enough just to adopt the sitting or kneeling position that is essential for the proper appreciation of a Japanese domestic interior. Traditional features such as the *tokonoma* (an alcove for the display of a picture scroll and perhaps a vase with a single flower), the *tana* (ornamental, asymmetrical shelves) and the *shoin* (window and study place) have ancient functional origins but long ago became purely symbolic. Westerners admire their strangeness as much as their beauty. And there was an irrationality in the Japanese house that is baffling to the western mind, for example the apparent refusal to employ the principle of triangulation, either in the roof structure or the bracing of walls. The removable external walls and the deep shadows of the interior created a cool, well-ventilated refuge in hot, wet summers, but in freezing winters the whistling draughts and non-existent thermal insulation made padded outer garments and woolly underwear absolutely essential. The only artificial source of heat was the *hibachi,* a metal-lined box containing a few pieces of glowing charcoal used not to raise the air temperature but as a personal heater on the principle of the hot-water bottle. And then there is the strangeness of the Japanese garden, inseparable from the house and designed to be viewed from it as if it were a picture not too different from the scroll in the *tokonoma*. The garden represented nature, but was anything but spontaneous or wild. Just as there were pattern books for houses, there were pattern books for gardens. For each standard

Tea house in the garden of the Katsura Villa, Kyoto.

type or style of garden there was a recommended arrangement of stone, tree, lantern and pool. No space was too small to become a garden because of that curious Japanese attitude to scale which delights in converting a six foot by three foot patch into a dream of infinite space.

And finally there was the influence of the tea ceremony, a ritual that originated in Zen Buddhist monasteries in the twelfth century but became a cult in its own right in the sixteenth century and gave rise not just to a new building type but to a whole architectural style and aesthetic sensibility. The tea houses in the garden of the Katsura Villa in Kyoto are little more than rustic huts, yet they are among the most important 'monuments' of Japanese architecture.

Detached wooden houses with traditional pan-tiled roofs are still plentiful in the outer suburbs of Japanese cities. They are built by the inheritors of the great carpentry tradition and they still use versions of old techniques and details, although the timber is increasingly likely to be pre-cut by computer-controlled machinery. Traditional ways of domestic life – sitting and sleeping on the floor – survive and it is common for new houses to include a *tatami* room. But for the most part, western ways have been adopted and the traditional house in its pure form has disappeared. Western furniture and air conditioning have undermined the logic of the Japanese house. It is passing into history. But this doesn't mean that it should cease to be an inspiration for the designers and producers of modern houses. In the era of 'lean production' and 'mass

A traditional Japanese house of the twentieth century.

customization', the rigidity of the Kiwari system seems less relevant to western house building now than it did 40 years ago. But efficiency is not the only reason for standardization. The modesty, simplicity and austerity of the traditional Japanese house remains a shining example, even if the Japanese themselves pay little heed to it. The lesson of the Japanese house is summed up in an ancient text by an early master of prefabrication, the twelfth-century poet and recluse Kamo-no-Chomei. This is how he describes his little house, hidden in the mists of Mount Ohara:

> It is a cottage of quite a peculiar kind, for it is only ten feet square and less than seven feet high and as I did not decide to fix it in any definite place I did not choose the site by divination as usual. The walls are of rough plastered earth and the roof is of thatch. All the joints are hinged with metal so that if the situation no longer pleases me, I can easily take it down and transport it elsewhere. And this can be done with very little labour, for the whole will fill only two cart loads, and beyond the small wage of the carters nothing else is needed.[9]

# Conclusion

This is not a government report. There will be no list of recommendations for action. But it might be worthwhile to summarize the lessons that architects could learn from the prefabricated house.

Architecture draws much of its prestige from its linguistic association with all that is solid and reliable. Foundation, cornerstone, structure, bastion – building metaphors like these reflect back on architecture and lend it a certain moral authority. Lightweight panels and prefabrication are an affront to architecture's dignity. If this seems far-fetched, consider the very common architectural habit of insisting on the 'honest expression' of materials and structure, the rule that bans imitation brickwork and insists that oak beams must be made of real oak (except that ideally they should be steel beams because technology has advanced and demands to be honestly expressed). The rule doesn't stand up to historical or theoretical scrutiny and should be quietly ditched. According to Gottfried Semper, the transfer of form from one material to another is an essential part of architecture's 'cosmogonic' or world-making function. Panels and boxes have their own dignity and their own theoretical justifications.

Authorship is another source of prestige in architecture, and another dubious concept fundamentally challenged by the special requirements of the prefabricated house. Building is essentially a collaborative enterprise, even more so when it moves into the factory. The design of a semi-standard product, even a relatively primitive one like a house, cannot be the work of one person. Factory managers, production engineers, buyers, accountants, marketing people, shop-floor workers, lorry drivers – all are potential collaborators in the design. Of course there must be somebody in charge, and that person could well be an architect, but he or she will not be the author of the design in the same way that a painter is the author of a painting. Even more important than collaboration with fellow producers is collaboration with consumers. The one-off house for a sympathetic patron does not provide an appropriate model for the relationship between designer and buyer of a prefabricated house. There is no scope for that bullying tempered by charm that architects like Frank Lloyd Wright specialized in. The customer is not an individual but a market sector and the house must have general appeal. For most market sectors, this means that it must speak the common language of domestic architecture that everybody understands. Architects should respect that language and learn to use it gracefully. Wilful, individual creations will be rejected, and appeals to architectural theory will be futile.

Architecture's sensitivity to the nuances of 'place' is admirable in its way but it has become a fetish, especially in schools of architecture. The idea that the form of a building should emerge naturally from the unique combination of factors generated by a particular client and a particular site is appealing but unrealistic. Most houses are standard products adaptable to almost any site. There is nothing wrong with this. It has always been so. Vernacular architecture, the only kind that everybody loves, is an architecture of standard construction details applied to standard building types.

The distinction between constructional design and spatial design is an important one. Architects commonly assume responsibility for both and treat them as if they were of equal value. The house building industry knows otherwise. A building technology, whether developed over centuries or invented in a factory, is a precious thing in which much practical ingenuity has been invested. It takes real experts to develop a building technology, preferably with hands-on knowledge of the materials involved and tools used to shape them. New technologies designed in isolation on the drawing board are very unlikely to be successful. Technologies have to be developed, not designed, and you need a factory to develop them in. Anyway, it's usually safer and cheaper to adapt an old technology. Most prefabricated house technologies are essentially versions of the 170-year-old American balloon frame. In contrast to constructional design, spatial design is cheap. Almost anybody can do it, which is why designs for house types are given away by the hundred in pattern books. Nobody knows or cares who designed them. Architect-designed house plans undoubtedly work better and are nicer to live in, but that won't necessarily make them more valuable. Architects should stop despising pattern books and learn to use them to their advantage.

Volume house builders who are quite content to string their standard types along suburban streets without any professional help, will often turn to an architect when faced with an awkward site and higher planning density. Reconciling the demands of prefabrication with the complexities of urban sites and multistorey buildings is the sort of thing that architects do well. Le Corbusier's Immeubles-Villas project of 1925 was essentially a production run of Esprit Nouveau pavilions stacked up to form a slab block. Each apartment had a double-height living-room and a garden at the side, and there was plenty of scope for customization. If you preferred you could just buy one pavilion and site it in the suburbs as a detached house. The project was never realized, but its time may have come. At a recent London exhibition, Terrapin Buildings erected a single modular show flat on the ground. With its clay tile cladding and its umbrella roof it made a handsome little house.

Prefabrication has long been associated with systems of one kind or another: closed systems, open systems, dimensionally co-ordinated systems. Systems are themselves a kind of architecture, abstract mathematical constructs that their creators find completely absorbing. But architects who dream of the perfect system should heed the terrible warning of the Packaged House, Konrad Wachsmann's bid to solve post-war America's housing crisis. His system was almost perfect. An ingenious standard connector and a limited range of lightweight panels seemed to be all that was needed to produce an infinite range of smart, co-ordinated buildings. But Wachsmann wasn't really interested in building the buildings. He was only interested in the system. And like a character in a tragic fable, in the end he couldn't let his baby go out into the world. It was his system and he couldn't share it: better that the whole enterprise come crashing down than that the perfection of the system be violated. Systems are essentially utopian. They aspire to a perfect state, putting an end to change and development. But successful industrial products don't stay the same. There is always an improved model waiting in the wings. That's why authorship is irrelevant. It is only when the useful life of the product is over and it has made its way into a museum that anyone thinks to ask who designed it.

Since Wachsmann's day the twin revolutions of 'lean production' and computer-aided manufacture (not necessarily connected) have transformed modern industry. Mass production of the old, Fordist kind is dead and all the old assumptions about industrial production have died with it. Architects used to call on those assumptions as excuses to stay out of the factory. The argument went something like this: Factories make thousands of identical units like Model T Fords, all black. That is what factories are for. So if you want to prefabricate buildings, you must standardize them and mass produce them. But this is impossible, for various reasons: the market is too small to justify the investment; all building sites are unique so all buildings have to be different; besides, buildings are not complicated pieces of engineering like cars – they don't have to travel along at 40 miles per hour, they just have to stay put and keep the weather out. So prefabrication isn't worth it. In any case, it would only result in a built environment of mind-numbing monotony. Buildings are better made on site, not in factories. End of argument.

But then Taichii Ohno of Toyota came along and demonstrated that factory-made products, even complicated ones like cars, did not all have to be identical. The factory could adapt and, within limits, make whatever the customer wanted. The arrival of numerically controlled machines and CAD/CAM technology made customization even easier. The assembly line was still moving, but the products on it were all different. For the Japanese, this was enough to justify a massive investment in prefabricated houses; not cheap, temporary buildings, but high-quality, up-market industrial products. The assumption that prefabrication, standardization and mass production were three aspects of the same industrial imperative was called into question. The irony is, however, that the imperative had never applied to simple products like houses in the first place. The mobile home industry in the US had been successfully producing factory-made, customized homes for years without knowing anything about lean production or CAD/CAM.

Prefabrication does not necessarily imply either mass production or standardization. In fact none of the three terms necessarily implies the other two. Standardization is not essential and mind-numbing monotony is not inevitable. Customers can participate in the design of their house, at least to the extent of choosing from a range of options as they do when they buy a car. On the other hand, standardization is not necessarily a bad thing. It has virtues of its own quite apart from any considerations of efficiency or economy. People like standard products that are tried and tested and available from stock. They see them around and they covet them. The man next door might have one. The perfect customization system would be as futile and unnecessary as the perfect planning grid. Offering customers a choice is one thing; asking them to design the whole building from scratch quite another. The best chances of success probably lie somewhere between the universal system at one extreme and the 'take it or leave it' single house type at the other. A range of models, each with a range of options might be a sensible strategy.

It should be borne in mind too that the house is not necessarily a single entity. In 1932 Frank Lloyd Wright imagined an 'assembled house' to which extra ready-made rooms could be added when the owner could afford it. Ultra-frame's neo-Victorian conservatories are not often spoken of in the same breath as Frank Lloyd Wright, but the idea is the same, and they are a commercial reality whereas Wright's project was never realized.

It is tempting to conclude by simply calling for a greater involvement of architects in prefabricated housing, and of course that is the general message of this book. But it seems more important to emphasize what prefabrication has already achieved without the help of architects. Those achievements should be respected: the balloon frame, the mail-order house, the mobile

Käpylä Garden Suburb, Helsinki, 1920–25.

home, the modular hotel, the self-build house kit. If this list begins to conjure up an image of a world despoiled by tacky boxes, reflect that it needn't be so. Prefabricated wooden houses built in the 1920s and '30s on the outskirts of Gothenburg, Stockholm and Helsinki now frame wonderfully mature living environments. Prefabricated buildings can be temporary or permanent, cheap or expensive, all the same or all different, small or large, traditional or modern, well designed or badly designed. They are not intrinsically mean or base and they do not necessarily make soulless places. A garden shed can be more enchanting than a luxury villa; a roadside restaurant can be as pleasant as a pavilion in a park. It is a question of judgement, of caring about the building and its future life, of knowing how to strike the right balance between standard products and special places. Architects ought to be good at this kind of thing. But designing one-off prototypes to amuse their colleagues will get them nowhere. To make a real difference, they must learn the lesson of the prefabricated house.

# References

## Introduction

1 Garry Stevens, *The Favored Circle* (Cambridge, MA, 1998).

## Chapter 1

1 The most recent edition of *Towards a New Architecture* is to be found in *Essential Le Corbusier: L'Esprit Nouveau Articles* (Oxford, 1998).
2 Tim Benton, '*Citrohan 1 and 2*', in *Le Corbusier, Architect of the Century*, exh. cat., Arts Council of Great Britain, Hayward Gallery, London (1987), p. 208.
3 *Towards a New Architecture*, p. 137.
4 Gilbert Herbert, *The Dream of the Factory-made House* (Cambridge, MA, 1984).
5 Konrad Wachsmann, *Building the Wooden House: Technique and Design*, with new contributions by Christa and Michael Gruning, and Christian Sumi (Basel, 1995).
6 Tom Wolfe, *From Bauhaus to our House* (New York, 1981).
7 *The Dream of the Factory-made House*, p. 275.
8 Konrad Wachsmann, *Wendepunkt im Bauen* (Wiesbaden, 1959); Eng. trans. as *The Turning Point of Building* (New York, 1961), p. 9.
9 Ibid., p. 140.
10 Ibid., p. 154.
11 R. Buckminster Fuller and Robert W. Marks, *The Dymaxion World of Buckminster Fuller* (Garden City, NY, 1973), p. 36.
12 John McHale, *R. Buckminster Fuller* (London, 1962), p. 26; Martin Pawley, *Buckminster Fuller* (New York, 1990), p. 107. See also H. Ward Jandl, *Yesterday's Houses of Tomorrow* (Washington, DC, 1991), Chapter 5.
13 Bruce Brooks Pfeiffer, ed., *Frank Lloyd Wright, Collected Writings*, III (New York, 1993), pp. 123–5.
14 *Frank Lloyd Wright, Collected Writings*, III, p. 203.
15 Henry-Russell Hitchcock, *In the Nature of Materials* (New York, 1947), p. 94.
16 John Sergeant, *Frank Lloyd Wright's Usonian Houses* (New York, 1976), p. 145.

17 Benedikt Huber and Jean-Claude Steinegger, eds, *Jean Prouvé* (Zurich, 1971), p. 189.

18 Charlotte Ellis, 'Prouvé's Prefabs', *Architects' Journal* (3 April 1985), pp. 46–51.

19 *Jean Prouvé*, pp. 194–6.

20 Beatriz Colomina, 'Reflections on the Eames House', in *The Work of Charles and Ray Eames* (New York, 1997), p. 132 and note 11.

21 The fullest summary of Archigram projects is in *Archigram* (New York, 1999).

22 *Archigram*, pp. 14–15.

23 Martin Pawley, *Theory and Design in the Second Machine Age* (Oxford, 1990), p. 87.

## Chapter 2

1 Sigfried Giedion, 'American Development in Design', *New Directions*, IV (1939), pp. 167–79.

2 Sigfried Giedion, *Space, Time and Architecture*, 5th edn (London, 1967), pp. 347–55.

3 Walker Field, 'A Re-examination into the Invention of the Balloon Frame', *Journal of the Society of Architectural Historians*, II/4 (October 1942), pp. 3–29.

4 Horace Greely, *Great Industries of the United States* (Hartford, CT, 1872), p. 40; quoted in Walker Field, 'Re-examination', p. 24.

5 Gilbert Herbert, *Pioneers of Prefabrication* (London, 1978), Chapter 2.

6 Charles E. Peterson, 'Prefabs in the California Gold Rush, 1849', *Journal of the Society of Architectural Historians* (December 1965), pp. 318–24.

7 Herbert, *Pioneers of Prefabrication*, p. 66.

8 Katherine Cole Stevenson and H. Ward Jandl, *Houses by Mail: A Guide to Houses from Sears, Roebuck and Company* (Washington, DC, 1986), p. 25.

9 *Houses by Mail*, p. 21.

10 H. Ward Jandl, *Yesterday's Houses of Tomorrow* (Washington, DC, 1991), p. 166.

11 'Prefabrication Gets its Chance', *Architectural Forum* (February 1942), pp. 81–3.

12 Burnham Kelly, *The Prefabrication of Houses* (Cambridge, MA, 1951), p. 59.

13 'Snapshot of an Infant Industry', *Architectural Forum* (February 1942), pp. 84–8.

14 Kelly, *The Prefabrication of Houses*, p. 60.

15 Ibid., p. 68.

16 The fullest accounts of the Lustron house are: *Yesterday's Houses of Tomorrow*, Chapter 12; and Floyd E. Barwig, 'Lustron Homes', in Richard Bender, *A Crack in the Rear View Mirror* (New York, 1973), pp. 58–61.

17 See R. B. White, *Prefabrication: A History of its Development in Great Britain* (London 1965), Part 2.

18 Brenda Vale, *Prefabs: A History of the UK Temporary Housing Programme* (London, 1995), p. 106–10.

19 John Madge, ed., *Tomorrow's Houses* (London, 1946), p. 206.

20 Vale, *Prefabs*, p. 2 and p. 26, note 2.

21  See White, *Prefabrication*, Part 3.
22  Brian Finnimore, *Houses from the Factory* (London, 1989).
23  *Tomorrow's Houses*, pp. 118, 137.
24  Finnimore, *Houses from the Factory*, p. 181.
25  Ibid., Appendix 6, p. 273.
26  David Birkbeck, 'Who Really Remembers', *Building Homes*, 7 (July 1999), pp. 36–8.

## Chapter 3

1  The standard history of the mobile home is Alan D. Wallis, *Wheel Estate* (New York, 1991).
2  Arthur D. Bernhardt, *Building Tomorrow* (London, 1980), p. 29.
3  Wallis, *Wheel Estate*, pp. 125–32.
4  John Steinbeck, *Travels with Charley* (New York, 1962, repr. 1997), pp. 74–80.
5  John Fraser Hart, Michelle J. Rhodes and John T. Morgan, eds, *The Unknown World of the Mobile Home* (Baltimore, MD, 2002), pp. 49–52.
6  See Manufactured Housing Institute, *Urban Design Project* (2001).
7  Bernhardt, *Building Tomorrow*, p. 205.
8  Ibid., p. 80.
9  *Archigram* (New York, 1999), p. 59.
10  'A Mobile Home by Any Other Name', *Architectural Record* (April 1968), p. 145.
11  'The Mobile Home is the 20th Century Brick', *Architectural Record* (April 1968), p. 142.
12  Manufactured Housing Institute, *Understanding Today's Manufactured Housing*, p. 1 (Source of statistics: US Department of Commerce, Bureau of the Census).

## Chapter 4

1  Roland Barthes, 'The Death of the Author', in Stephen Heath, ed., *Image, Music, Text* (London, 1984).
2  Tim Benton, 'Monastery of Sainte-Marie de la Tourette', in *Le Corbusier, Architect of the Century*, exh. cat., Arts Council of Great Britain, Hayward Gallery, London (London, 1987), p. 250.
3  Nouritza Matossian, *Xenakis* (London, 1986), pp. 68–9.
4  Robert Furneaux Jordan, *Le Corbusier* (London, 1972), p. 143.
5  Colin Rowe, 'Dominican Monastery of La Tourette', *Architectural Review* (June 1961), p. 408.
6  Derek Sugden, 'The Sugden House: Dreaming and Living', in Helen Webster, ed., *Modernism without Rhetoric* (London, 1997).
7  'House in Lincolnshire', *Domus* (November 1995), pp. 36–41.
8  Sergison Bates Architects, *Papers* (London, 2001), pp. 40–41.

## Chapter 5

1 René Descartes, *Discourse on Method*, in Margaret D. Wilson, ed., *The Essential Descartes* (London 1969), p. 121.
2 Martin Heidegger, *Building, Dwelling, Thinking*, in David Farrell Krell, ed., *Basic Writings, Martin Heidegger* (London, 1993), p. 348.
3 John Ruskin, *The Seven Lamps of Architecture* (London, 1880, repr. New York, 1989), p. 35.
4 Gottfried Semper, *The Four Elements of Architecture and Other Writings*, trans. Harry Francis Mallgrave and Wolfgang Herrmann (Cambridge, 1989).
5 John Summerson, *Architecture in Britain, 1530–1830*, 9th edn (London, 1993), p. 63.

## Chapter 6

1 The memorandum is quoted in full in 'Gropius at Twenty-Six', *Architectural Review* (July 1961), pp. 49–51.
2 Sigfried Giedion, *Mechanization Takes Command* (New York, 1948), p. 78.
3 Alfred Farwell Bemis and John Burchard, *The Evolving House* (Cambridge, MA, 1933–6).
4 Andrew Saint, *Towards a Social Architecture* (London, 1987), p. 30.
5 Quoted in Barry Russell, *Building Systems, Industrialisation and Architecture* (London, 1981), p. 306.
6 Chris Abel, 'Ditching the Dinosaur Sanctuary', in *Architecture and Identity* (London, 1997), p. 7.
7 J. F. Eden, 'Metrology and the Module', *Architectural Design*, XXXVII/13 (1967), pp. 148–50.
8 Quoted in CIRIA, *Standardisation and Pre-Assembly* (London, 1999), p. 136.
9 *Standardisation and Pre-Assembly*, p. 173.
10 Colin Davies, *High Tech Architecture* (London, 1988), p. 7.
11 Paul Barker, 'Sorry, but we don't want to live in flats', *New Statesman* (30 September 2002), pp. 46–7.
12 Kent Larson, 'A Machine Crafted Home of the Future', *A+U* (October 2000), pp. 60–67.

## Chapter 7

1 The Housing Forum, *Homing in on Excellence: A Commentary on the Use of Off-site Fabrication Methods for the UK Housebuilding Industry* (London, n.d.), p. 15.
2 Deborah S. Ryan, *The Ideal Home through the 20th Century* (London, 1997), p. 58.
3 Office of the Deputy Prime Minister, *Sustainable Communities: Building for the Future* (London, 2003), p. 38.

## Chapter 8

1 Jonathan Glancey, 'Don't even think about swinging a cat', *The Guardian* (27 August 2001).
2 Gus Alexander, 'Pees in a Pod', *Building* (7 May 1999), p. 33.
3 See Martin Pawley, 'The Other Systems Men', *Building Design* (18 March 1983), pp. 26–9.
4 BRE Centre for Sustainable Construction, *Prefabricated Housing in the UK, a Case Study: Murray Grove, Hackney* (2001).
5 UK Department of the Environment, Transport and the Regions, *Rethinking Construction* (1998).
6 See Allison Arieff and Bryan Burkhardt, *Prefab* (Layton, UT, 2002).

## Chapter 9

1 James Barlow and Ritsuko Ozaki, Department of Trade and Industry, *Japanese Lessons on Customer-Focused Housebuilding* (2001), p. 9.
2 Edward S. Morse, *Japanese Homes and their Surroundings* (London, 1885, repr. New York, 1961).
3 Kevin Nute, *Frank Lloyd Wright and Japan* (London, 1993), Chapter 2.
4 Frank Lloyd Wright, *A Testament* (1957), p. 205, quoted in *Frank Lloyd Wright and Japan*, p. 4.
5 Bruno Taut, *Houses and People of Japan* (London, 1936).
6 Tetsuro Yoshida, *Japanese House and Garden* (New York, 1955).
7 Walter Gropius, 'Foreword', in Heinrich Engel, *The Japanese House: A Tradition for Contemporary Architecture* (Rutland, VT, 1964).
8 Engel, *The Japanese House*, p. 57.
9 *The Ten Foot Square Hut and Tales of the Heike*, trans. A. L. Sadler (Sydney, 1928), p. 13.

# Select Bibliography

Abel, Chris, *Architecture and Identity: Responses to Cultural and Technological Change* (Oxford, 2000)

Arieff, Allison, *Prefab* (Salt Lake City, 2002)

Banham, Reyner, *Theory and Design in the First Machine Age* (Oxford, 1962)

Bemis, Albert Farwell, *The Evolving House* (Cambridge, MA, 1933–6)

Bender, Richard, *A Crack in the Rear View Mirror* (New York, 1973)

Bernhardt, Arthur D., *Building Tomorrow* (London, 1980)

Callicott, Nick, *Computer-aided Manufacture in Architecture* (Oxford, 2001)

Cook, Peter, ed., *Archigram* (New York, 1999)

Davies, Colin, *High Tech Architecture* (New York, 1988)

——, *Hopkins: The Work of Michael Hopkins and Partners* (London, 1993)

Engel, Heino, *Measure and Construction of the Japanese House* (Rutland, VT, 1985)

Finnimore, Brian, *Houses from the Factory* (London, 1989)

Frampton, Kenneth, *Studies in Tectonic Culture: The Poetics of Construction in Nineteenth and Twentieth Century Architecture* (London, 1995)

Gann, David M., *Building Innovation: Complex Constructs in a Changing World* (London, 2000)

Giedion, Sigfried, *Mechanization Takes Command* (New York, 1948)

——, *Space, Time and Architecture* (London, 1967)

Hart, John Fraser, Michelle J. Rhodes and John T. Morgan, *The Unknown World of the Mobile Home* (Baltimore, 2002)

Herbert, Gilbert, *The Dream of the Factory-made House* (London, 1984)

——, *Pioneers of Prefabrication: The British Contribution in the Nineteenth Century* (Baltimore, 1978)

Hitchcock, Henry-Russell, *In the Nature of Materials: The Buildings of Frank Lloyd Wright* (New York, 1942)

Huber, Benedikt, and Jean-Claude Steinegger, eds, *Jean Prouvé: Industrial Architecture* (Zurich, 1971) [French, German and English texts]

Jandl, H. Ward, *Yesterday's Houses of Tomorrow: Innovative American Homes 1850 to 1950* (Washington, DC, 1991)

Katz, Peter, *The New Urbanism: Toward an Architecture of Community* (New York, 1994)

Kelly, Burnham, *The Prefabrication of Houses* (Cambridge, MA, 1951)

Lambot, Ian, ed., *Norman Foster, Foster Associates: Buildings and Project*, III: *1978–1985* (Hong Kong, 1989)

Le Corbusier, *Vers une architecture* (Paris, 1923; Eng. trans., London, 1927); repr. in *Essential Le Corbusier: L'Esprit Nouveau Articles* (Oxford, 1998)

McHale, John, R., *Buckminster Fuller* (London, 1962)

McAlester, Virginia, and Lee McAlester, *A Field Guide to American Houses* (New York, 1984)

Matossian, Nouritza, *Xenakis* (London, 1986)

Nute, Kevin, *Frank Lloyd Wright and Japan* (London, 1993)

Pawley, Martin, *Buckminster Fuller* (London, 1990)

——, *Terminal Architecture* (London, 1998)

——, *Theory and Design in the Second Machine Age* (Oxford, 1990)

Pevsner, Nikolaus, *An Outline of European Architecture* (London, 1963)

Raeburn, M., and V. Wilson, eds, *Le Corbusier: Architect of the Century*, exh. cat., Hayward Gallery, London (London, 1987)

Russell, Barry, *Building Systems, Industrialization and Architecture* (London, 1981)

Russell, Frank, ed., *Richard Rogers and Partners* (London, 1985)

Ryan, Deborah, *The Ideal Home through the 20th Century: Daily Mail Ideal Home Exhibition* (London, 1997)

Saint, Andrew, *Towards a Social Architecture: The Role of School Building in Post-war England* (London, 1987)

Sergeant, John, *Frank Lloyd Wright's Usonian Houses* (New York, 1976)

Steele, James, *Eames House: Charles and Ray Eames* (London, 1994)

Stevens, Garry, *The Favored Circle: The Social Foundations of Architectural Distinction* (London, 1998)

Stevenson, Katherine Cole, and H. Ward Jandl, *Houses by Mail: A Guide to Houses from Sears, Roebuck and Company* (Washington, DC, 1986)

Stickley, Gustav, ed., *Craftsman Bungalows: 59 Homes from 'The Craftsman'* (London, 1988)

Summerson, John, *Architecture in Britain, 1530 to 1830* (London, 1993)

Tetsuro, Yoshida, *The Japanese House and Garden* (London, 1969)

Vale, Brenda, *Prefabs: A History of the UK Temporary Housing Programme* (London, 1995)

Wachsmann, Konrad, *Building the Wooden House: Technique and Design* (Basel, 1995)

White, R. B., *Prefabrication: A History of its Development in Great Britain* (London, 1965)

——, *The Turning Point of Building: Structure and Design* (New York, 1961)

Wallis, Allan D., *Wheel Estate: The Rise and Decline of Mobile Homes* (New York, 1991)

Womack, James P., and Daniel T. Jones, *Lean Thinking* (London, 1996)London London

# Acknowledgements

London Metropolitan University gave financial support to this project, for which I am very grateful. I would like to thank the following experts who helped me with my research: Mary Albright of Border Oak, Simon Allford, Andy Atkins of Portakabin, Roy Bentley of the BP/Bovis Global Alliance, John Blyde, Richard Cottrell, Lars Emvik, David Gann, Rex Henry, Richard Lavington, Rory McCabe, Ian McKay of Welcome Break, Robert Millerchip, Nigel Morris, Paul Newman, Mike Parkhurst of Skyline, James Pickard, Michael Stacey, Jamie Thompson, Brian Vermeulen, Nick Whitehouse of Terrapin and Dan Ziebarth of Palm Harbor Homes. Research in Japan was made easy and enjoyable by the generous hospitality of Masaaki Dozen and Nobuko Ueda of National Panahome, Takumi Katayama of Daiwa, and Rika Nagatomo of Sekisui Chemical. Special thanks are due to Jane King, to Ward and Jean Belford for inviting me into their Florida home, to Andrew Mead for help with pictures, to Robert Harbison for his constant encouragement and to my wife, Sue Wallington, for her loving support and sensible advice.

# Photographic Acknowledgements

The author and publishers wish to express their thanks to the below sources of illustrative material and/or permission to reproduce it (in some cases locations are also given below):

Picture material courtesy of the author: pp. 17, 35, 38, 47, 50, 70, 72, 74, 91 (top), 92, 97, 99, 101, 111, 112, 124, 125, 126, 131, 145, 150, 151, 153 (middle and foot), 159, 160, 165, 166, 170, 171, 172, 174, 178, 180, 182, 183, 189, 190, 192, 195, 200, 210; photos © Archigram Achives 2004: pp. 40, 41, 42; from Albert Farwell Bemis, *The Evolving House*, vol. 3 (New York: Random House, 1936): p. 135 (top); photo Broderbund: p. 128; photo Martin Charles: p. 34; photo courtesy of Heino Engel: p. 197; EMAP/Architectural Press Archive: p. 18 (photo Peter Davey), 28, 45, 58, 62, 63, 64 (photo Dell & Wainwright), 65, 68, 76 (top, photo Michael Lorant; foot, photo Eric de Maré), 79, 85, 103 (photos William Toomey), 136, 137 (photo William Toomey), 138 (photo Building Research Station); Fondation Le Corbusier: pp. 12, 15; photos © Fondation Le Corbusier/ADAGP, Paris and DACS, London 2005): p. 12, 14, 15, 16; photo:© Pedro E. Guerrero: p. 32; from Gilbert Herbert, *The Dream of the Factory Made House* (Cambridge, MA: MIT Press, 1984): p. 21; from Gilbert Herbert, *Pioneers of Prefabrication* (Baltimore and London: Johns Hopkins University Press, 1978): p. 48; photo courtesy of Richard Horden's office: p. 39; from H. Ward Jandl, *Yesterday's Houses of Tomorrow* (Washington, DC: Preservation Press, 1991): p. 55; photo G.E. Kidder Smith, courtesy of the Kidder Smith Library (Kidder Smith Collection), Rotch Visual Collections, Massachusetts Institute of Technology, Cambridge, Mass.: p. 86; Kingspan Group PLC: p. 149; from Joachim Krausse and Claude Lichtenstein, eds, *Your Private Sky: R. Buckminster Fuller* (Zurich: Lars Mueller Publishers, 1999): p. 26; Kunstmuseum Basel (gift of Dr Raoul de la Roche), photo Martin Bühler: p. 14; photo Jean-Charles Liess: p. 91 (foot); photo courtesy of m-house: p. 184 (top); photo Manufactured Housing Institute and Susan Maxman and Partners: p. 81; Department of Architecture, MIT: p. 146; from Edward S. Morse, *Japanese Homes and their Surroundings* (Boston, 1886): p. 194; photo National

Panahome: p. 187; photo Omar Park Homes: p. 184 (foot); photo courtesy of Richard Rogers Partnership: p. 37; from Deborah Ryan, *The Ideal Home through the Twentieth Century* (Hazar Publishing: London, 1977): p. 161; photo Sergison Bates Architects: p. 105; photo © HYPERLINK "http://www.smoothe.co.uk" www.smoothe.com: p. 176; photo courtesy of Space4: p. 164.

# Index